The Authorities

Powerful Wisdom from Leaders in the Field

DENNIS GARRIDO
Bringing Balance to Your Life

Copyright © 2017 Authorities Press

ISBN: 978-1-77277-163-3

All rights reserved. No portion of this book may be reproduced mechanically, electronically, or by any other means, including photocopying, without permission of the publisher or author except in the case of brief quotations embodied in critical articles and reviews. It is illegal to copy this book, post it to a website, or distribute it by any other means without permission from the publisher or author.

Limits of Liability and Disclaimer of Warranty

The author and publisher shall not be liable for your misuse of the enclosed material. This book is strictly for informational and educational purposes.

Warning – Disclaimer

The purpose of this book is to educate and entertain. The author and/or publisher do not guarantee that anyone following these techniques, suggestions, tips, ideas, or strategies will become successful. The author and/or publisher shall have neither liability nor responsibility to anyone with respect to any loss or damage caused, or alleged to be caused, directly or indirectly by the information contained in this book.

Medical Disclaimer
The medical or health information in this book is provided as an information resource only, and is not to be used or relied on for any diagnostic or treatment purposes. This information is not intended to be patient education, does not create any patient-physician relationship, and should not be used as a substitute for professional diagnosis and treatment.

Publisher
Authorities Press
Markham, ON
Canada

Printed in Canada and the United States of America

FOREWORD

Experts are to be admired for their knowledge, but they often remain unrecognized by the general public because they save their information and insights for paying customers and clients. There are many experts in a given field, but their impact is limited to the handful of people with whom they work.

Unlike experts, authorities share their knowledge and expertise far more broadly, so they make a big impact on the world. Authorities become known and admired as leading experts and, as such, typically do very well economically and professionally. Most authorities are also mature enough to know that part of the joy of monetary success is the accompanying moral and spiritual obligation to give back.

Many people want to learn and work with well-respected and generous authorities, but don't always know where to find them. They may be known to their peers, or within a specific community, but have not had the opportunity to reach a wider audience. At one time, they might have submitted a proposal to the For Dummies or Chicken Soup for the Soul series of books, but it's now almost impossible to get accepted as a new author in such branded book series.

It is more than fitting that Raymond Aaron, an internationally known and respected authority in his own right, would be the one to recognize the need for a new venue in which authorities could share their considerable knowledge with readers everywhere. As the only author ever to be included in both of the book series mentioned above, Raymond has had the opportunity to give back and he understands how crucial it is for authorities to have a platform from which to share their expertise.

I have known and worked with Raymond for a number of years and consider him a valued friend and talented coach. He knows how to spot talented and knowledgeable people and he desires to see them prosper. Over the years, success coaching and speaking engagements around the world have made it possible for Raymond to meet many of these talented authorities. He recognizes and relates to their passion and enthusiasm for what they do, as well as their desire to share what they know. He tells me that's why he created this new nonfiction branded book series, *The Authorities*.

Dr. Nido Qubein
President, High Point University

TABLE OF CONTENTS

Introduction...V

Bringing Balance to Your Life 1
Dennis Garrido

Branding Small Business................................11
Raymond Aaron

Happiness: How to Experience the "Real Deals" 25
Marci Shimoff

Sex, Love and Relationships...........................35
Dr. John Gray

You are Born to Have Joy 41
Lykke Stjernswärd

Purpose and Living Your Passion Cure 51
Ron Bell

Break Through Your Barriers & Live Your Dreams 71
Sandra Westland

Create the Life of Your Dreams 81
Dexter Montgomery & Pamela Montgomery

A Dream Life for the Asking 91
Tom Barber

Awakening Your Healer Within 101
Philip Young

Honor Your Inner Treasures 119
Celina Tio

The Secret to Words 137
Jacqueline Lucien

INTRODUCTION

This book introduces you to *The Authorities* — individuals who have distinguished themselves in life and in business. Authorities make a big impact on the world. Authorities are leaders in their chosen fields. Authorities typically do very well financially, and are evolved enough to know that part of the joy of monetary success is the accompanying social, moral and spiritual obligation to give back.

Authorities are not just outstanding. They are also *known* to be outstanding.

This additional element begins to explain the difference between two strategic business and life concepts — one that seems great, but isn't, and the other that fills in the essential missing gap of the first.

The first concept is "the expert."

What is an expert? The real definition is …

EXPERT: *a person who knows stuff*

People who have attained a very senior academic degree (like a PhD or an MD) definitely know stuff. People who read voraciously and retain what they read definitely know stuff. Unfortunately, just because you know stuff does not mean that anyone respects the fact that you do. Even though some experts are successful, alas, most are not — because knowing stuff is not enough.

Well, then, what is the missing piece?

What the expert lacks, "the authority" has. The authority both knows stuff and is *known* to know stuff. So, more simply …

AUTHORITY: *a person who is known as an expert*

The difference is not subtle. The difference is not merely semantic. The difference is enormous.

When it comes to this subject, there are actually three categories in which people fall:

- People who don't know much and are unsuccessful in life and in business. Most people fall in this category.

- People who know stuff, but still don't leave much of a footprint in the world. There are a lot of people like this.

- Experts who are also *known* as experts become authorities and authorities are always wondrously successful. Authorities are able to contribute more to humanity through both their chosen work and their giving back.

This book is about the highest category, *The Authorities* — people who have reached the peak in their field and are known as such.

While you will recognize some of *The Authorities* in this book such as Raymond Aaron, there is a new generation of Authorities rising and our featured author Dennis Garrido is one of them.

Coming from a troubled past and many years in the foster care system, Dennis has great compassion and the ability to be able to help others overcome imbalance in their life and to see the growth that they desire.

In *The Authorities*, you will learn the steps you need to take to not only identify the imbalances in your life, but also bring balance through having both your needs and your wants met.

To be considered for inclusion in a subsequent edition of *The Authorities*, register to attend a future event at www.aaron.com/events where you will be interviewed and considered.

Bringing Balance to Your Life

DENNIS GARRIDO

When I woke up in the hospital staring up into the terrified eyes of someone I cared about, after my second cardiac arrest in one year, I knew that things had to change in my life. Especially because I was only in my twenties at the time.

Everything in my life was out of balance. Obviously, physically because I was lying in the emergency room, but more importantly my mind, emotions, and spirit were completely out of whack, and that had taken a toll on my body.

Now you may be wondering how someone so young could have had two cardiac arrests before the age of 30? It won't be hard to imagine once I share my story with you. I wish I could tell you that I had a great upbringing, one filled with laughter and love, but it wasn't.

At age eleven I was removed from my parent's home by The Children's Aid Society because they deemed my parents unfit to raise me. During that time, I went through a whirlwind of emotions. A part of me was happy that change was finally occurring, because clearly at that point, the way things were, wasn't working at all.

Another part of me felt fear because of the unknown. I didn't know exactly where I would be living, nor did I know for sure what my group & foster homes would be like, what the other kids would be like, what the living conditions would be like, how far or close I'd be to my family and hometown, etc. Essentially, I wasn't 100% certain nor 100% convinced that I was going into better circumstances.

Also, I felt sad, since I wouldn't see my parents or siblings anymore, nor my home town and many of the people whom I'd see on a regular basis; everything FAMILIAR would be gone! Lastly, I felt angry, that it had come to me being removed from my parent's house, away from those who were in my life for all those years. As twisted and messed up as it may be, I was angry that I was leaving a life that I had become accustomed to and felt somewhat comfortable in (comfortable in comparison to the unknown that lay ahead); and most of all, angry that I was leaving FAMILIARITY!!!!

Please understand me, I am no longer angry at my parents, and you shouldn't be either. They did the best they could, but when you are broken yourself, unless you find a way out, you will repeat what had been bestowed on you from the previous generations. I can be thankful because what I went through helped create the person I am today and as a coach, it gives me great empathy and understanding to be able to help others. So, don't feel sorry for me because even though my life had a rough start, I get to choose the rest of it and it is going to be GREAT!!!

THE NEXT SEVEN YEARS OF MY LIFE

For the next seven years until I turned 18, I was bounced from foster/group home to foster/group home. I rarely spent more than three months at any one place, and it caused some major emotional setbacks that took me a long time to overcome.

One of the biggest negative emotional setbacks was again to do with familiarity. As I spent time with those at my new home, seeing them every day and coming to know them personally; I naturally formed a connection/friendship with them. It seemed that no sooner had I done that; they were removed from my life. People whom I really liked (a few of them, whom I loved), ALL GONE!!! Which basically solidified my already ingrained defence mechanism of keeping distant from others; not allowing anyone to get close enough to form any connection with me.

Inevitably, this made it very difficult for me to form any type of relationship with anyone. School and extracurricular activities were hard because I never knew how long I would be staying in one place. What was the point of making friends if I could never keep them? It was a lot easier to keep my distance than to reach out yet again and have everything torn away from me.

Eventually, I started to tear down the wall that prevented me from getting too close to anyone. To this day, the negative emotional setbacks I experienced, still affect me to some degree; though I CHOOSE not to allow them to prevent me from forming meaningful relationships!

THE DARKEST TIME OF MY LIFE

All that change led to one of the darkest periods of my life. Emotionally and mentally I had shut down and could no longer function. Life was so hard. Even things that were simple, now became agonizingly difficult and it hit the point where I didn't want to live anymore. What was the use of carrying on in this horrible life when there wasn't any hope of it changing?

My life began to narrow down to one permanent solution, and that was to end it all by committing suicide. I just couldn't handle life anymore, but I truly believe that Almighty God, the universe or whatever you want to call it, had a bigger plan for me. Even though I tried several times, I just couldn't die!!! Because of those attempts, I ended up in psychiatric institutions, a few times.

It finally came to the point where I was tired of trying to die, I was tired of institutions and I was weary from all the self-harm, and so I came to a decision. I guess you could say that it was a turning point in my life; I wasn't going to attempt suicide anymore. I wasn't sure what to do because my circumstances hadn't changed, but I was willing to look for options. That was the beginning point of change in my life. The will to live!!!

IT DIDN'T GET BETTER RIGHT AWAY

Life is a journey with twists, hills, and valleys of varying shapes and sizes, with occasional points where you make decisions that put you on a different path. The determination not to kill myself had set me on a new road, but I still didn't know what to do or which way to go. It was slow going as I fumbled my way through, but at least I was moving forward!!!

At age 18 I was no longer in the custody of The Children's Aid Society, so, I moved back with my parents, which was the perfect testing grounds for me to apply the life lessons I had learned so far. You would be amazed by how much maturity one can have at 18 when you have been through what I have. It wasn't easy, and it was hard work, but I managed to re-establish a relationship with my parents and not only complete high school, but also graduate from post-secondary schooling.

One of the things I had decided to do was get my student loans paid off in the six-month grace period, which I managed to do; but in doing so, I pushed myself way beyond my physical limits which brought on the first cardiac arrest.

You would think I would have learned from that first experience, but I didn't, and less than a year later we are back to the beginning of this chapter waking up in the hospital from my second one.

This time I learned my lesson and chose a different path, but I still didn't know how to achieve what I needed. For so long I had lived in imbalance, that I didn't know where to start, but the catalyst for change was just around the corner.

I FINALLY REALIZED WHAT BALANCE WAS

Believe it or not, it is the simplest things that can bring about the most profound changes in life. My search for balance in my life had begun, and it is amazing how the answer came; by a knock at my door one day.

That day I was busy working on something, so when the first knock came, I ignored it. It was only after a couple of rings of the doorbell that I finally decided that I would answer it. There was a well-dressed gentleman at the door and even though I don't remember most of what he said, one thing became clear, I was missing an essential element to finding the balance I craved. Now, I knew what it was. You can only find balance when you address ALL the areas of your life, and I had been missing one. The spiritual side.

It is amazing what happens when you finally have all the pieces together. As I started to study the Bible, I finally could build a solid spiritual foundation, that enabled me to re-evaluate things in my life, and thus, put a plan together to create balance in my life. In the rest of this chapter, I am going to share with you what I learned.

Just before I do that, I do want to mention one thing. All of this is a process. Can I say that I am 100% balanced in my life? No, but when I started at 3-4% and then jumped to 85%, I think that is very good growth. It's difficult to attain 100% balance in every aspect of one's life, that is why even the most successful people keep learning and growing. So, the goal is not perfection, but growth. As long as you are continuing to move forward, that is all that matters.

7 STEPS TO BRING BALANCE TO YOUR LIFE

Here's one of the things that I have learned about bringing balance to your life. In some ways, it is easy. The steps I am going to teach you are simple to understand. The hard part is training yourself to be aware of it every day and live by it. The good thing is, though it may be hard at first, the more you practice it, the easier it gets.

STEP 1

Ask yourself, "What are my priorities in life?" You want to look at it from all aspects of your life, personal and professional. In terms of personal that includes goals physically, emotionally, mentally, spiritually, relationships (such as your spouse or significant other), family and friends. You want to look at it from the point of what you need and what you want. For each one, you should have one to two priorities.

In terms of professional, they can include your current work situation and areas of improvement there, plus plan for your future. Put down both needs and wants.

	NEEDS	WANTS
PERSONAL		
PROFESSIONAL		

STEP 2

Look at your needs column. What are the most important priorities personally and professionally? It is important that you only start out working on a few at a time. If you try to do everything at once, you will become overwhelmed and quit. Then, figure out the things you need to do to get those needs met.

STEP 3

Now go through your wants and do the same thing as Step 2 above. Don't overlook this. Part of having balance in life is having both your needs and wants met. Obviously, your needs are more important, but without the wants, you give up hope.

STEP 4

Set up a timeline for those needs to be accomplished. What are you going to do today, this week, this month, this year, and in the next five years to bring yourself to reach those priorities?

STEP 5

Do the same thing for your wants. Set up your timeline of completion.

STEP 6

DO THE ACTIONS. Here is where the rubber meets the road. You can plan and plan and plan, but if there is no action involved you will be in the same place, with the same problems, five years from now.

STEP 7

Re-evaluate. Every few months go back through this whole process again.

As you grow and change, so will your priorities, your needs and your wants.

THE BEST WAY TO ACCOMPLISH THIS

Very rarely can a person accomplish this alone. Have you ever heard the saying, "You can't see the forest for the trees?" That is what happens in our lives. We get so caught up in the unimportant things right in front of us, that we miss the big picture and we don't recognize growth when it occurs.

Now, you do have several options. One is to have family members try to help you through this. While you do need their support, they are usually looking at the same trees you are and can miss things.

Two, you can go to friends for help. They do tend to see more of the big picture, but many times they can't give you the encouragement and motivation you need at times to get past yourself.

Three, you work with a professional who knows how to help you bring balance to your life. They can come alongside of you and guide you to the quickest path to success because there will be obstacles that try to stop you. Did I forget to mention that?

No road to balance is smooth; little pebbles will get into your shoes to irritate you and take your focus off your goals. Barriers will be put up that you will have to learn how to go over, under, around or through. People will get in your way and tell you that it is the wrong road to take and you should follow them. All sorts of things will try to keep you from what you want.

Coaches are keen observers who can not only help you with what is going on right now, but they have been down your road and they know what is up ahead and can keep you moving forward, even when everything is telling you to stop.

That is what I'm offering to be for you. Let me help you on your path to balance in your life. I have been on both sides of the coin, and I can guide you through the roughest parts. I can relate to what you are feeling and am more than willing to help you navigate this wonderful thing called life.

First of all, if you would like more information on how to start this process, you can pre-order my upcoming book at www.dennisgarrido.com Second, you can email me at dennis@dennisgarrido.com and request your free 15-minute phone consultation where we can discuss your situation and see if we are a good fit for each other. Third, maybe you realize more people need to hear this message. I am also available to speak to groups and conferences. If so, just send me an email, and we can arrange a time to speak.

No matter what you decide, know this. You can achieve balance in your life. It is possible. I can tell you that it has been worth everything I went through to get to this point. The peace I experience now, compared to the chaos I lived before, is so amazing and I wish the same for you.

Don't miss out. Make the choice to change your life today, and I guarantee that you won't regret it!!!

Branding Small Business

RAYMOND AARON

Branding is an incredibly important tool for creating and building your business. Large companies have been benefiting from branding ever since people first started selling things to other people. Branding made those businesses big.

If you're a small business owner, you probably imagine that small companies are different and don't need branding as much as large companies do. Not true. The truth is small businesses need branding just as much, if not more, than large companies.

Perhaps you've thought about branding, but assumed you'd need millions of dollars to do it properly, or that branding is just the same thing as marketing. Nothing could be further from the truth.

Marketing is the engine of your company's success. Branding is the fuel in that engine.

In the old days, salespeople were a big part of the selling process. They recommended one product over another and laid out the reasons why it was better. Salespeople had credibility because they knew about all the products, and customers often took the advice they had to offer.

Today, consumers control the buying process. They shop in big box stores, super-sized supermarkets, and over the Internet — where there are no salespeople. Buyers now get online and gather information beforehand. They learn about all the products available and look to see if there really is any difference between them. Consumers also read reviews and check social media to see if both the company and the product are reputable. In other words, they want to know what the brand is all about.

The way of commerce used to be: "Nothing happens till something is sold." Today it's: "Nothing happens till something is branded!"

DEFINING A BRAND

A brand is a proper name that stands for something. It lives in the consumer's mind, has positive or negative characteristics, and invokes a feeling or an image. In short, it's a person's perception of a product or a company.

When all goes well, consumers associate the same characteristics with a brand that the company talks about in its advertising, public relations, marketing and sales materials. Of course, when a product doesn't live up to what the company says about it, the brand gets a bad reputation. On the other hand, if a product or service over-delivers on the promises made, the brand can become a superstar.

RECOGNIZING BRANDING AND ITS CHARACTERISTICS

Branding is the science and art of making something that isn't unique, unique. Branding in the marketplace is the same as branding on a ranch. On a ranch, ranchers use branding to differentiate their cattle from every other rancher's cattle (because all cattle look pretty much the same). In the marketplace, branding is what makes a product stand out in a crowd of similar products. The right branding gets you noticed, remembered and sold — or perhaps I should say bought, because today it is all about buying, not selling.

There are four main characteristics of branding that make it an integral part of the marketing and purchasing process.

1. Branding makes you trustworthy and known

Branding makes a product more special than other products. With branding, a normal, everyday product has a personality, and a first and last name, and people know who you are.

In today's marketplace, most products are, more or less, just like their competition. Toilet paper is toilet paper, milk is milk, and a grocery store by any other name is still a grocery store. However, branding takes a product and makes it unique. For example, high-quality drinking water is available from just about every tap in the Western world and it's free, but people pay good money for it when it comes in a bottle. Branding takes bottled water and makes Evian.

Furthermore, every aspect of your brand gives potential customers a feeling or comfort level that they associate with you. The more powerful and positive that feeling is, the more easily and more frequently they will want to do business with you and, indeed, will do business with you.

2. Branding differentiates you from others

Strong branding makes you better than your competition, and makes your product name memorable and easy to remember. Even if your product is absolutely the same as every other product like it, branding makes it special. Branding makes it the first product a consumer thinks about when deciding to make a purchase.

Branding also makes a product seem popular. Everyone knows about it, which implicitly says people like it. And, if people like it, it must be good.

3. Branding makes you worth more money

The stronger your branding is, the more likely people are willing to spend that little bit extra because they believe you, your product, your service, or your business are worth it. They may say they won't, but they will. They do it all the time.

For example, a one-pound box of Godiva chocolates costs about $40; the same weight of Hershey's Kisses costs about $4. The quality of the chocolate isn't ten times greater. The reason people buy Godiva is that the brand Godiva means "gift" whereas the brand Hershey means "snack". Gifts obviously cost more than snacks.

4. Branding pre-sells your product

In the buying age, people most often make the decision on which products to pick up before they walk into the store. The stronger the branding, the more likely people are to think in terms of your product rather than the product category. For example, people are as likely, maybe even more likely, to add Hellmann's to the shopping list as they are to write down simply mayo. The same is true for soda, ketchup, and many other products with successful, strong branding.

Plus, as soon as a shopper gets to the shelf, branding can provide a quick reminder of what products to grab in a few ways:

- An icon or logo
- A specific color
- An audio icon

BRANDING IN A SMALL BUSINESS

Big companies spend millions of dollars on advertising, marketing, and public relations (PR) to build recognition of a new product name. They get their selling messages out to the public using television, radio, magazines, and the Internet. They can even throw money at damage control when necessary. The strategies for branding are the same in a small business, but the scale, costs, and a few of the tactics change.

Make your brand name work harder

The name of a small business can mean everything in terms of branding. Your brand name needs to work harder for your business than you do. It's the first thing a prospective customer sees, and it is how they will remember you. A brand name has to be memorable when spoken, and focused in its meaning. If the name doesn't represent what consumers believe about a product and the company that makes it, then that brand will fail.

In building your product's reputation and image, less is often significantly more. Make sure the name you choose immediately gives a sense of what you do.

Large corporations have millions of dollars to take a meaningless brand name and make it stand for something. Small businesses don't, so use words that really mean something. Strive for something interesting and be right on point. You don't need to be boring.

Plumbers, for example, would do well setting themselves apart with names like "The On-Time Plumber" or "24/7 Plumbing". The same is true for electricians, IT providers, or even marketing consultants. Plenty of other types of business are so general in nature they just don't work hard enough in a business or product name.

Even the playing field: The Net

The Internet has leveled the playing field for small businesses like nothing else. You can use the Internet in several ways to market your brand:

Website: Developing and maintaining a website is easier than ever. Anyone can find your business regardless of its size.

Social Media: Facebook and Twitter can promote your brand in a cost-effective manner.

BUILDING YOUR BRAND WITH THE BRANDING LADDER

Even if you do everything perfectly the first time (and I don't know anyone who does), branding takes time. How much time isn't just up to you, but you can speed things along by understanding the different levels of branding, as well as the business and marketing strategies that can get you to the top.

Introducing the Branding Ladder

Moving through the levels of branding is like climbing a ladder to the top of the marketplace. The Branding Ladder has five distinct rungs and, unlike stairs, you can't take them two at a time. You have to take them in order, and some businesses spend more time on each rung than others.

You can also think of the Branding Ladder in terms of a scale from zero to ten. Everyone starts at zero. If you properly climb the ladder, you can end up at 12 out of 10. The Branding Ladder below shows a special rung at the top of the ladder that can take your business over the top. The following section explains the Branding Ladder and how your small business can move up it.

THE BRANDING LADDER	
Brand Advocacy	12/10
Brand Insistence	10/10
Brand Preference	3/10
Brand Awareness	1/10
Brand Absence	0/10

Rung 1: Living in the void

Your business, in fact every business, starts at the bottom rung, which is called brand absence, meaning you have no brand whatsoever except your own name. On a scale of one to ten, brand absence is, of course, zero. That's the worst place to live and obviously the most difficult entrepreneurially. The good news is that the only way is up.

Ninety-seven percent of businesses live on this rung of the Branding Ladder. They earn far less than they want to earn, far less than they should earn, and far less than they would earn if they did exactly the same work under a real brand.

Rung 2: Achieving awareness

Brand awareness is a good first step up the ladder to the second rung. Actually, it's really good, especially because 97 percent of businesses never get there. You want people to be aware of you. When person A speaks to person B and says, "Have you heard of "The 24/7 Plumber?" You want the answer to be "yes".

On that scale of one to ten, however, brand awareness is only a one. It's better than nothing, but not that much better. Although people know of your brand, being aware doesn't mean that they are interested in buying it. Coca Cola drinkers know about Pepsi, but they don't drink it.

Rung 3: Becoming the preferred brand

Getting to the third rung, brand preference, is definitely a real step up. This rung means that people prefer to use your product or service rather than that of your competition. They believe there is a real difference between you and others, and you're their first choice. This rung is a crucial branding stage for parity products, such as bottled water and breakfast cereals, not to mention plumbers, electricians, lawyers, and all the others. Brand preference is clearly better than brand awareness, but it's less than halfway up the ladder.

Car rental companies represent a perfect example of why brand preference may not be enough. When someone lands at an airport and needs to rent a car on the spot, he or she may go straight to the preferred rental counter. If that company has a car available, it's a sale. However, if all the cars for that company have been rented, the person will move to the next rental kiosk without much thought, because one rental car is just as good as another.

Exerting Brand Preference needs to be easy and convenient

If all you have is brand preference, your business is on shaky ground and you can lose business for the feeblest of reasons. Very few people go to a second or third supermarket just to find their favorite brand of bottled water. Similarly, a shopper may prefer one store over another but, if both stores sell the same products, he or she will often go to the closest store even if it is not the better liked one. The reason for staying nearby does not need to be a dramatic one — the shopper may simply be tired, on a tight schedule, or not in the mood to travel.

Rung 4: Making it you and only you

When your customers are so committed to your product or service that they won't accept a substitute, you have reached the fourth rung of the Branding Ladder. All companies strive to reach this place, called brand insistence.

Brand insistence means that someone's experience with a product in terms of performance, durability, customer service, and image has been sufficiently exceptional. As a result, the product has earned an incredible level of loyalty.

If the product isn't available where the customer is, he or she will literally not buy something else. Rather, the person will look for the preferred product elsewhere. Can you imagine what a fabulous place this is for a company to be? Brand insistence is the best of the best, the perfect ten out of ten, the whole ball of wax.

Apple is a perfect example of brand insistence

Apple users don't just think, they know in their heads and hearts, that anything made by Apple is technologically-advanced, user-friendly, and just all-around superior. Committed to everything Apple, Mac users won't even entertain the thought that a PC may have positive attributes.

Apple people love everything about their Macs, iPads, iPhones, the Mac stores and all those apps. When the company introduces a new product, many of its brand-insistent fans actually wait in line overnight to be one of the first to have it. Steve Jobs is one of their idols.

Considering one big potential problem

Unfortunately, you can lose brand insistence much more quickly than you can achieve it. Brand-insistent customers have such high expectations that they can be disillusioned or disappointed by just one bad product experience. You also have to consistently reinforce the positives because insistence can fade over time. Even someone who has bought and re-bought a specific brand of car for the last 20 years can decide it's just time for a change. That's how fickle the world is.

At ten out of ten, brand insistence may seem like the top rung of the ladder, but it's not. One rung is actually better, and it involves getting your brand-insistent customers to keep polishing your brand for you.

Rung 5: Getting customers to do the work for you

Brand advocacy is the highest rung on the ladder. It's better than ten out of ten because you have customers who are so happy with your product that they want everyone to know about it and use it. Think of them as uber-fans. Not only do they recommend you to friends and family, they also practically shout your praises from the rooftops, interrupt conversations among strangers to give their opinion, and tell everyone they meet how fantastic you are. Most companies can only aspire to this level of customer satisfaction. Apple is one of the few large corporations in recent history that has brand advocates all over the world.

- Brand advocacy does the following five extraordinary things for your company. Brand advocacy:

- Provides a level of visibility that you couldn't pay for if you tried. Brand advocates are so enthusiastic they talk about you all the time, and reach people in ways general media and public relations can't. You get great visibility because they make sure people actually listen.

- Delivers free advertising and public relations. Companies love the extra super-positive messaging, all for free.

- Affords a level of credibility that literally can't be bought. Brand advocates are more than just walking testimonials. They are living proof that you are the best.

- Provides pre-sold prospective customers. Advocate recommendations carry so much weight that they are worth much more than plain referrals. They deliver customers ready and committed to purchasing your product or service.

- Increases profits exponentially. Brand advocates are money-making machines for your business because they increase sales and decrease marketing costs.

For these reasons, brand advocacy is 12 out of 10!!

BRANDING YOURSELF: HOW TO DO SO IN FOUR EASY WAYS

If you're interested in branding your product or company, you may not be sure where to begin. The good news: I'm here to help. You can brand in many ways, but here I pare it down to four ways to help you start:

Branding by association

This way involves hanging out with and being seen with people who are very much higher than you in your particular niche.

Branding by achievement

This way repurposes your previous achievements.

Branding by testimonial

This way makes use of the testimonials that you receive but have likely never used.

Branding by WOW

A WOW is the pleasantly unexpected, the equivalent of going the extra mile. The easiest and most certain way to WOW people is to tell them that you've written a book. To discover how you can write a book of own, go to www.BrandingSmallBusinessForDummies.com.

Happiness: How to Experience the "Real Deals"

MARCI SHIMOFF

I was 41 years old, stretched out on a lounge chair by my pool and reflecting on my life. I had achieved all that I thought I needed to be happy.

You see, when I was a child, I thought there would be five main things that would ensure that I'd be happy: a successful career helping people, a loving husband, a comfortable home, a great body, and a wonderful circle of friends. After years of study, hard work, and a few "lucky breaks," I finally had them all. (Okay, so my body didn't quite look like Halle Berry's—but four out of five isn't bad!) You think I'd have been on the top of the world.

But surprisingly I wasn't. I felt an emptiness inside that the outer successes of life couldn't fill. I was also afraid that if I lost any of those things, I might be miserable. Sadly, I knew I wasn't alone in feeling this way.

While happiness is the one thing we all truly want, so few people really experience the deep and lasting fulfillment that fills our soul. Why aren't we finding it?

Because, in the words of the old country western song, we're looking for happiness in "all the wrong places."

Looking around, I saw that the happiest people I knew weren't the most successful and famous. Some were married, some were single. Some had lots of money, and some didn't have a dime. Some of them even had health challenges. From where I stood, there seemed to be no rhyme or reason to what made people happy. The obvious question became: *Could a person actually be happy for no reason?*

I had to find out.

So I threw myself into the study of happiness. I interviewed scores of scientists, as well as 100 unconditionally happy people. (I call them the Happy 100.) I delved into the research from the burgeoning field of positive psychology, the study of the positive traits that enable people to enjoy meaningful, fulfilling, and happy lives.

What I found changed my life. To share this knowledge with others, I wrote a book called *Happy for No Reason: 7 Steps to Being Happy from the Inside Out*.

One day, as I sat down to compile my findings, all the pieces of the puzzle fell into place. I had a simple, but profound "a-ha"—there's a continuum of happiness:

Unhappy: We all know what this means: life seems flat. Some of the signs are anxiety, fatigue, feeling blue or low—your "garden-variety" unhappiness. This isn't the same as clinical depression, which is characterized by deep despair and hopelessness that dramatically interferes with your ability to live a normal life, and for which professional help is absolutely necessary.

Happy for Bad Reason: When people are unhappy, they often try to make themselves feel better by indulging in addictions or behaviors that may feel good in the moment but are ultimately detrimental. They seek the highs that come from drugs, alcohol, excessive sex, "retail therapy," compulsive gambling, over-eating, and too much television-watching, to name a few. This kind of "happiness" is hardly happiness at all. It is only a temporary way to numb or escape our unhappiness through fleeting experiences of pleasure.

Happy for Good Reason: This is what people usually mean by happiness: having good relationships with our family and friends, success in our careers, financial security, a nice house or car, or using our talents and strengths well. It's the pleasure we derive from having the healthy things in our lives that we want.

Don't get me wrong. I'm all for this kind of happiness! It's just that it's only half the story. Being Happy for Good Reason depends on the external conditions of our lives—these conditions change or are lost, our happiness usually goes too. Relying solely on this type of happiness is where a lot of our fear is stemming from these days. We're afraid the things we think we need to be happy may be slipping from our grasp.

Deep inside, I think we all know that life isn't meant to be about getting by, numbing our pain, or having everything "under control." True happiness doesn't come from merely collecting an assortment of happy experiences. At our core, we know there's something more than this.

There is. It's the next level on the happiness continuum—Happy for No Reason.

Happy for No Reason: This is true happiness—a state of peace and well-being that isn't dependent on external circumstances.

Happy for No Reason isn't elation, euphoria, mood spikes, or peak experiences that don't last. It doesn't mean grinning like a fool 24/7 or experiencing a superficial high. Happy for No Reason isn't an emotion. In fact, when you are Happy for No Reason, you can have *any* emotion—including sadness, fear, anger or hurt—but you still experience that underlying state of peace and well-being.

When you're Happy for No Reason, you *bring* happiness to your outer experiences rather than trying to *extract* happiness from them. You don't need to manipulate the world around you to try to make yourself happy. You live from happiness, rather than *for* happiness.

This is a revolutionary concept. Most of us focus on being Happy for Good Reason, stringing together as many happy experiences as we can, like beads in a necklace, to create a happy life. We have to spend a lot of time and energy trying to find just the right beads so we can have a "happy necklace".

Being Happy for No Reason, in our necklace analogy, is like having a happy string. No matter what beads we put on our necklace—good, bad or indifferent—our inner experience, which is the string that runs through them all, is happy, and creates a happy life.

Happy for No Reason is a state that's been spoken of in virtually all spiritual and religious traditions throughout history. The concept is universal. In Buddhism, it is called causeless joy; in Christianity, the kingdom of Heaven within; and in Judaism it is called *ashrei*, an inner sense of holiness and health. In Islam it is called *falah*, happiness and well-being; and in Hinduism it is called *ananda*, or pure bliss. Some traditions refer to it as an enlightened or awakened state.

So how can you be Happy for No Reason?

Science is verifying the way. Researchers in the field of positive psychology have found that we each have a "happiness set-point," that determines our level of happiness. No matter what happens, whether it's something as exhilarating as winning the lottery or as challenging as a horrible accident, most people eventually return to their original happiness level. Like your weight set-point, which keeps the scale hovering around the same number, your happiness set-point will remain the same **unless you make a concerted effort to change it.** In the same way you'd crank up the thermostat to get comfortable on a chilly day, you actually have the power to reprogram your happiness set-point to a higher level of peace and well-being. The secret lies in practicing the habits of happiness.

Some books and programs will tell you that you can simply decide to be happy. They say just make up your mind to be happy—and you will be.

I don't agree.

You can't just decide to be happy, any more than you can decide to be fit or to be a great piano virtuoso and expect instant mastery. You can, however, decide to take the necessary steps, like exercising or taking piano lessons—and by practicing those skills, you can get in shape or give recitals. In the same way, you can become Happy for No Reason through practicing the habits of happy people.

All of your habitual thoughts and behaviors in the past have created specific neural pathways in the wiring in your brain, like grooves in a record. When we think or behave a certain way over and over, the neural pathway is strengthened and the groove becomes deeper—the way a well-traveled route through a field eventually becomes a clear-cut path. Unhappy people tend to have more negative neural pathways. This is why you can't just ignore the realities of your brain's wiring and *decide* to be happy! To raise your level of happiness, you have to create new grooves.

Scientists used to think that once a person reached adulthood, the brain was fairly well "set in stone" and there wasn't much you could do to change it. But new research is revealing exciting information about the brain's neuroplasticity: when you think, feel and act in different ways, the brain changes and actually rewires itself. You aren't doomed to the same negative neural pathways for your whole life. Leading brain researcher Dr. Richard Davidson, of the University of Wisconsin says, "Based on what we know of the plasticity of the brain, we can think of things like happiness and compassion as skills that are no different from learning to play a musical instrument or tennis …. it is possible to train our brains to be happy."

While a few of the Happy 100 I interviewed were born happy, most of them learned to be happy by practicing habits that supported their happiness. That means wherever you are on the happiness continuum, it's entirely in your power to raise your happiness level.

In the course of my research, I uncovered 21 core happiness habits that anyone can use to become happier and stay that way. You can find all 21 happiness habits at www.HappyForNoReason.com

Here are a few tips to get you started:

1. **Incline Your Mind Toward Joy.** Have you noticed that your mind tends to register the negative events in your life more than the positive? If you get ten compliments in a day and one criticism, what do you remember? For most people, it's the criticism. Scientists call this our "negativity bias" — our primitive survival wiring that causes us to pay more attention to the negative than the positive. To reverse this bias, get into the daily habit of consciously registering the positive around you: the sun on your skin, the taste of a favorite food, a smile or kind word from a co-worker or friend. Once you notice something positive, take a moment to savor it deeply and feel it; make it more than just a mental observation. Spend 20 seconds soaking up the happiness you feel.

2. **Let Love Lead.** One way to power up your heart's flow is by sending loving kindness to your friends and family, as well as strangers you pass on the street. Next time you're waiting for the elevator at work, stuck in a line at the store or caught up in traffic, send a silent wish to the people you see for their happiness, well-being, and health. Simply wishing others well switches on the "pump" in your own heart that generates love and creates a strong current of happiness.

3. **Lighten Your Load.** To make a habit of letting go of worries and negative thoughts, start by letting go on the physical level. Cultural anthropologist Angeles Arrien recommends giving or throwing away 27 items a day for nine days. This deceptively simple practice will help you break attachments that no longer serve you.

4. **Make Your Cells Happy.** Your brain contains a veritable pharmacopeia of natural happiness-enhancing neurochemicals — endorphins, serotonin, oxytocin, and dopamine — just waiting to be released to every organ and cell in your body. The way that you eat, move, rest, and even your facial expression can shift the balance of your body's feel-good-chemicals, or "Joy Juice", in your favor. To dispense some extra Joy Juice — smile. Scientists have discovered that smiling decreases stress hormones and boosts happiness chemicals, which increase the body's T-cells, reduce pain, and enhance relaxation. You may not feel like it, but smiling — even artificially to begin with — starts the ball rolling and will turn into a real smile in short order.

5. **Hang with the Happy.** We catch the emotions of those around us just like we catch their colds — it's called emotional contagion. So it's important to make wise choices about the company you keep. Create appropriate boundaries with emotional bullies and "happiness vampires" who suck the life out of you. Develop your happiness "dream team" — a mastermind or support group you meet with regularly to keep you steady on the path of raising your happiness.

"Happily ever after" isn't just for fairytales or for only the lucky few. Imagine experiencing inner peace and well-being as the backdrop for everything else in your life. When you're Happy for No Reason, it's not that your life always looks perfect — it's that, however it looks, you'll still be happy!

By Marci Shimoff. Based on the New York Times bestseller *Happy for No Reason: 7 Steps to Being Happy from the Inside Out*, which offers a revolutionary approach to experiencing deep and lasting happiness. The woman's face of the *Chicken Soup for the Soul* series and a featured teacher in *The Secret*, Marci is an authority on success, happiness, and the law of attraction. To order *Happy for No Reason* and receive free bonus gifts, go to www.happyfornoreason.com/mybook.

Sex, Love and Relationships

DR. JOHN GRAY

Just as great sex is important to lasting love, good health is important to sex and relationships. About 12 years ago, I cured myself of early stage Parkinson's disease. The doctors were amazed, but my wife was even more amazed. She noted that our relationship and sex life had become dramatically better. It turns out that the natural supplements I used to reverse Parkinson's can also make you more attentive and loving in your relationship. At that point, I realized that good relationship skills alone were not enough to sustain love and passion for a lifetime.

I shared many insights gained from my 40 years' experience as a marriage counselor and coach in *Men Are From Mars, Women Are From Venus*. And while my insights go a long way towards helping men and women understand and support each other, good communication skills alone are not always enough. For better relationships, we not only need to be healthy, but we must also experience optimum brain function.

If you are tired, depressed, anxious, not sleeping well, or in pain, then certainly romantic feelings will become a thing of the past. My recovery from Parkinson's revealed to me the profound connection between the quality of our health and our relationships. This insight has motivated me, over the past twelve years, to research the secrets of optimum health as a foundation for lasting love.

These are health secrets that are generally not explored in medical school. In medical school, doctors are indoctrinated into the culture of examining the symptoms, identifying the sickness, and prescribing a drug to treat that sickness. They learn very little about how to be healthy or to sustain successful relationships.

There are no university courses entitled "Better Nutrition For Better Sex". Drugs sometimes save lives, but they also have negative side effects that do little to preserve the passion in a relationship. Ideally, drugs should be used as a last resort and 90% of our health plan should be drug free. From this perspective, the heath care crisis, as well as our high rate of divorce in America, is indirectly caused by our dependence on doctors and prescription drugs.

Most people have not even considered that taking prescribed drugs (even for the small stuff) can weaken their relationships, which in turn makes them more vulnerable to more disease. For example, if you are feeling depressed or anxious, a drug may numb your pain, but it does nothing to help you correct the cause of your problem. It can even prevent you from feeling your natural motivation to get the emotional support you need. In a variety of ways, our common health complaints are all expressions of two major conditions: our lack of education to identify and support unmet gender-specific emotional needs; and our lack of education to identify and support unmet gender-specific nutritional needs.

With an understanding of natural solutions that have been around for thousands of years, drugs are not needed to treat many common complaints. Some symptoms like low energy, weight gain, allergies, hormonal imbalance, mood swings, poor sleep, indigestion, lack of focus, ADD and ADHD, procrastination, low motivation, memory loss, decreased libido, PMS, vaginal dryness, muscle and joint pain, or the lack of passion in life and/or our relationships can be treated drug-free. By using drugs (even over-the-counter drugs) to treat these common complaints, our bodies and relationships are weakened, making us more vulnerable to bigger and more costly health challenges like cancer, diabetes, heart disease, auto-immune disease, dementia, and Alzheimer's. In simple terms, by handling the easy stuff (the common complaints) without doctors and drugs, we can protect ourselves from the big stuff (cancer, heart disease, dementia, etc.) We can be healthy and also enjoy lasting love and passion in our personal lives.

Even if you are taking anti-depressants or hormone replacement therapy, sometimes all it takes to stop treating the symptom is to directly handle the cause. With specific mineral orotates (something most people have never heard of) or omega three oil from the brains of salmon, your stress levels immediately drop and you begin to feel happy and in love again.

For every health challenge, we have explored the effects on our relationships, with as well as natural remedies that can sometimes produce immediate positive results. You can find these natural solutions to common health complaints for free at my website: www.MarsVenus.com.

What they don't teach in medical school is how to be healthy and happy without the use of drugs or hormone replacement. By refusing drugs and taking responsibility for your health, a wealth of new possibilities can become available to you. We are designed to be healthy and happy, and it is within our reach if we commit to increasing our knowledge.

New research regarding the brain differences in men and women reveals how specific nutritional supplements, combined with gender-specific relationship and self-nurturing skills, can stimulate the hormones of health, happiness and increased energy. Over the past 10 years in my healing center in California, I witnessed how natural solutions coupled with gender-specific relationship skills could solve our common health complaints without drugs. By addressing these common complaints without prescribed drugs, not only do we feel better, but our relationships have the potential to improve dramatically.

Ultimately the cause of all our common complaints is higher stress levels. Researchers around the world all agree that chronic stress levels in our bodies provide a basis for any and all disease to take hold. An easy and quick solution for lowering our stress reactions is specific nutritional support combined with gender-smart relationship skills. Extra nutritional support is needed because stress depletes the body very quickly of essential nutrients. When a car engine is running more quickly, it uses fuel more quickly. When we are stressed, we need both extra nutrients and extra emotional support. Understanding what we need to take and where to get it requires education. Every week day at www.MarsVenus.com I have a live daily show where I freely answer questions and provide this much-needed new gender-specific insight.

At www.MarsVenus.com, we are happy to share what we have learned for creating healthy bodies and positive relationships. You can find a host of natural solutions for common complaints and feel confident that you have the power to feel fully alive with an abundance of energy and positive feelings that will enrich all your relationships.

You are Born to Have Joy

Lykke Stjernswärd

Many of you dream to actualize your potential, but you do not always know how to do so. I say, free yourself from your fears, take personal responsibility, be open to individual transformation, choose an active existence and contribute to an evolving society. Stand up and stand tall to make those choices and decisions that empower you and support positive change that resonates throughout communities and across time throughout generations. Connect and create the opportunity to make a difference, and know the value you are adding to the world.

I encourage you to connect to the present moment because joy is right in front of us for the taking. When we are mindful, we understand that the only life we have is the one we are living in now, and it is in the moment, the now, that we can shape our future. Tremendous power arises from recognizing this simple truth – that you're born to have joy in your life and in your work, and that you are your own key to living with passion and to enjoying every day as a gift. You come naked to the world. It is within you to build what you want in life.

My book *Born to Have Joy: Steps to Living the Life of a Gypset* shows you how you can step out of the conventional, to create an unconventional positive, joy-filled life that takes you out from the ocean of sameness and to make you a celebrity in your own life.

A cross of two words, Gypsy and Jet Set and coined by Julia Chaplin, author of Gypset Travel, it refers to a semi-nomadic bohemian lifestyle, a spirit of pure freedom "which fuses the ease and carefree lifestyle of a gypsy with the sophistication of the jet set. Gypsetters are artists, surfers, designers and bon vivants who live and work around the globe, from Jose Ignacio, Uruguay and Ibiza, Spain to Montauk, New York," describes Chaplin in her book. If you are a Gypsetter, you will be living an entrepreneurial life, inspiring others to think different inside the box, enjoying a nonconformist lifestyle and setting up your own guidelines for innovative businesses.

A Gypset life is based on a philosophy that a good life is lived at any moment and anywhere and that joy is found not in collecting things, but in experiences – reading a book at sunset on a deserted beach, sharing a home-cooked meal on a rooftop under candlelight in Goa or blending into the local culture, speaking the local language and engaging in community projects. Travelling off the beaten track and immersing in local cultures is part and parcel of the

Gypset style. So is standing out, trusting that your vision is important to the world and that you have the creative power and influence to inspire joy in your life and in the life of your community.

There are many opportunities for joy, and the first step is to recognize that the only life you have is the one you have now. You can absolutely shape or reshape your future, but you do so, not from fear or overplanning, from anxiety or overdoing, it is in the present moment where you love the life that you live that you are your most powerful.

As a photographer, I focus on the light of my client's inner being: his or her visible heart. I've found that the moment they are in touch with their inner glow, their path ahead is illuminated. As an entrepreneur and a founding creator of 8value.com, along with my fellow design partners, we work with change-makers, creating their brands by expressing their values visually. What that means is that we help you to know your value and to create your own personal brand that integrates your values, which are fundamental to differentiating yourself from others, adding vitality to your business, creating success, and bringing joy to your clients.

As part of our service, we give visual form to these values and help you design promotional items such as creating holistic satin ribbon or silicone bracelets with inspiring sayings such as *"The cure for fear is love"* or *"To be is to live here and now."* Think of them as little vessels or holders of your values to widen your influence by spreading joy.

By raising the visibility of your values, by helping your build relationships of trust and anticipating innovative solutions, we empower you to be a change-maker that stands for vision, innovation and sharing. In 8value.com, we encourage you to thrive on your own talent, invest your own time and energy where you love to make a difference, find hideouts and people with the perfect vibe that resonate and align with your desires, values, thoughts and actions. As a change-maker with game-changing solutions, you can create in and invest in something new birthed from your innovative vision that contributes to gross national happiness, not just gross national product.

LIVING AS A LEADER IN A SPIRIT OF FREEDOM

I've created a simple map for you to live the life of goodwill in *"Born to have Joy"* with simple-to-follow steps plus supportive guidance on which is the related chakra to work on for each move forward. By fine-tuning the energy centers and ensuring that body, mind and spirit are in perfect balance, you optimize your health, which is integral to living this life of freedom. I show you exciting destinations, both within and without, where you can thrive and be at your most creative, to be the artist of your own life. Since this is a journey of transformation and inspiration, akin to shedding old skin, I also recommend the appropriate affirmation engraved on a lucky charm bracelet from my collection at femininsacre.net to help connect your heart to your desire and to amp up your positive vibes to attract what you desire.

Here is a summary of the 8 steps:
1. Trust, respect and create a new you
2. Spot the opportunities for Joy
3. Foster joy and vitality by doing and loving what pleases you
4. Trust that you can always access infinite resources within you
5. Embrace quality time
6. Indulge in vital moments
7. Be creative and laugh a lot
8. Invite joy into your secret garden

1. Trust, respect and create a new you.

This is a process of transformation to create visibility for yourself by finding your inner glow to light your path ahead. Decide what you want to do, knowing that your life has a finite end, and ensure you keep a healthy balance between mind, body and spirit. Empower yourself by respecting your need for space and do not be afraid to say no. Be your own genuine self to become the celebrity in your own life, create a life game plan and know that you are the key to your own success.

2. Spot Opportunities for Joy

Life is to be lived and engaged with in the present. You find joy in small things that matter such as a comforting hug or a friendly smile. You discover joy in building connections of the heart, working with others whom you trust and with whom you are in perfect harmony to create a common purpose to invest in something new for a great return on fun. Find something that contributes to happiness as well as to traditional economic measures of economic value.

On my own personal path, every day I choose three reasons for which to be grateful, to feel joy here and now, to love in the present and to live for the future.

3. Foster joy and vitality by doing and loving what pleases you.

Vitality is sourced in trust, and the key to building trust, the lack of which creates sadness, is transparency. Trust is fostered by loving in the present, each day experiencing the power of awareness of the moment. Invite a bright future into your life, one where you put in time and energy into something or somewhere you love making a difference. As a change maker, create an action plan, a life's game plan that builds on all these elements, that enhances joy and promotes vitality. Be celebratory, grab the momentum of the moment, bring colors into your life because if you love the life you live, you will live a life of love.

4. Trust that you can always access your infinite resources.

In your inner world, your emotions pose challenges, but you can make friends of your emotions by giving each of them a name. On my journey, there is no room for envy, but if an emotion like jealousy springs up, I regard it as a friend bearing a message, a warning that I should either adapt to the situation or let go of whatever it is I'm hanging onto too tightly. Whether you rely on therapy or creative pursuits such as writing to become acquainted with your emotions, trust in your intuition as your best guide. It is your personal radar, and it will never mislead you. By trusting my intuition to tell stories around the world through photography, I now have a chance to display and share what I see through the lens with love and compassion. My jewelry brand, Féminin Sacré TM, has given me a voice and connects me with my sisters in humanity.

Your life is yours to create, so create new opportunities and new challenges for yourself. I choose sport as the arena in which I find new ways to stretch myself, such as paragliding in Verbier or heli-skilling on untracked, pristine trails over steep cliffs in Le Petit Combin in the Swiss Alps. We all have it within us to be daredevils.

5. Embrace Quality Time

No matter where your Gypset life leads you, everyday remind yourself that positive thinking is the most untapped natural resource in the world, and it doesn't run out on you! Surround yourself with loving, positive vibes that nurture and foster creativity.

Invite love into your life, starting with your body, which is your temple. Every day open to daily awareness by performing a salutation to the sun and including the ones you love and yourself in daily prayers. Such simple but heartfelt steps immersed in gratitude are easily introduced into your own life to support you, to maximize your health, to tap fully into your potential. Remember, the most thrilling way to enjoy life is to be the best part of yourself.

6. Indulge in Vital Moments

Schedule time for yourself, but also allocate time to at least three to five essential projects in your life. Like the legs of a chair, even if one falls off, the chair is still usable on three legs. If one of your projects fail to take off, you have at least 2 to 3 others working for you.

In other moments, cultivate a winning attitude. My own winning attitude is rooted in a belief in an intelligent design that is mightier than me. Being told "God loves me" and "I will pray for your both" are some of the most impactful words I have ever heard. What is your winning attitude? Find clues by taking responsibility for your thoughts and actions, build positive dialogue and ensure that your actions have a beautiful quality. Be mindful with your actions, be open, cool, sophisticated and purposeful.

7. Be creative and laugh a lot

'Creativity is intelligence having fun' - Albert Einstein

In Toltec wisdom, life is considered as art. You are the artist and your life, every aspect of it, every act, every day, every moment, is an expression of yourself as an artist. If your life is a blank canvas, what will you paint on it?

Where will you live? Find the cities and countries that fuel your creativity, spur your mobility and celebrate your freedom.

I suggest to you as a guide the books of Bobo Karlsson, a Swedish author now resident in Rio de Janeiro, who has been dubbed "Sweden's best urbanista". In his two books, *Urban Safari* and *Urban Safari 2*, he writes about his favorite cities and describes the souls and energies of cities such as Mexico City, whose mayor won the World Mayor Prize in 2010 for radically reducing pollution and improving the environment, and Berlin, whose mayor, Klaus Wowereit attracted the young to his city by creating the mantra "Penniless and Sexy". Cities have energies. Find the one that activates the creativity in your DNA.

8. Invite Joy into Your Own Secret Garden

Your secret garden is the little place in your heart where you spend time in to regain your equilibrium. Sometimes, you need a little help from outside to help you connect with your own secret garden. In Geneva, I use a unique transformational massage, Tulayoga, at Insens to heal myself with the help of my body.

You grow your secret garden by living with passion. Every day, laugh and dance, invite people into your life by hosting events that celebrate living. Join the party by linking the world for a worthy cause, meet new people and create new opportunities for yourself. In the words of Doña Esra, Toltec Wisdom teacher, "You have the right to be happy."

I've shared with you a little of the know-how so you can live a freedom and passion-fuelled life, one in which you are the star of your own show. I hope I've raised the bar for excitement to show that you can live free and create new change-making empowering opportunities while feeling fully confident you have access to unlimited resources to attract what you desire into your life. By shedding the stories that put you down, by filling the space with a winning attitude, by encouraging you to take responsibility for your thoughts and action, by linking to others with positive vibes, I assure you life as a Gypset is yours for the taking.

A lucky dreamer, explorer, photographer, entrepreneur and author, Lykke Stjernswärd has certainly lived up to her name, which means 'Happy Star Sword' in Swedish. A graduate of the Art Center College of Design in Switzerland and the University of Geneva she holds a B.A. in Communication Design and another in entrepreneurship and business development. With an international portfolio of photography, Lykke has worked on assignments for *Vogue* Nippon and her portraits have been published in *The New York Times* and *The Herald Tribune*. Her work is seen across the globe in London, Budapest, Hong Kong, Stockholm, Geneva and Riga, as well as on www.lykke.ch. Lykke's offers holistic fashion jewelry, bracelets and charms at www.femininsacre.net. She is also the founder of www.8value.com, a company that serves to brand visionary and innovative change-makers.

To discover how you can love success in your life and believe it is transferable, go to www.borntohavejoy.com

Purpose and Living Your Passion Cure

RON BELL

This chapter is about Ron Bell's defining your *Purpose and living your Passion Cure*. It offers 10 powerful ways to discover true inner peace and happiness. However, in order to understand each step in this process, we need to begin with two basic definitions.

First we'll look at the word purpose. Purpose is the reason for which something is done or created or for which something exists. Some useful synonyms are motive, motivation, cause, occasion, reason, basis, justification. When used as a verb, purpose is one's intention or objective. It has such synonyms as: intend, mean, aim, plan, design, decide, resolve, determine, propose, aspire. For example, I know someone who gets up every morning and purposefully begins to work on his goals at 6 am. He does not stop until 4 pm. He has a plan, the resolve to fulfill it and the motivation to meet all challenges. In other words, while his day is filled with purpose he also has a purpose.

Next we'll define the word passion. Passion is strong and barely a controllable emotion. The man in the previous example works, plays and rests on purpose. He is driven. The emotions he feels are strong, sometimes barely controllable; he needs to move through his days with a sense of purpose, resolve and determination. He is filled with passion.

The first question that begs to be asked, of course, is how do you get to such a place? How do you get on purpose and become motivated to stay there? One step is to begin with an inventory of your strengths. The way to do this is to ask yourself a series of questions. Ask yourself a question and the mind will always answer. Always. For example: Are you loyal? Do you pursue your assignments with pertinacity? Why do you act the way you do when faced with difficulty? Are you courageous? Honest? What are your greatest assets? Write your answers down on a piece of blank paper. Do you act on purpose throughout the day? How about passion—do you act with and feel great emotion that drives you forward toward your purpose, a passion that takes your strengths and carries them toward perfection? Create a list of the resources you, as an individual, possess and that you can get behind both mentally and emotionally.

There's wisdom in knowing your strengths: Men or women who know their strengths are never without resources. They can turn to this tool box whenever some difficulty or trouble passes through their lives. Your strengths can be the difference between staying on task (or purpose) and falling back into the rut that most people live in. This is why it's so important to combine purpose and passion. Acting on purpose from minute to minute depends completely on your motivation, and your motivation is very much about passion. The greater your emotional investment in your action, the greater will be that which drives you. Think of passion as the gas that runs the car of purpose. You can't go anywhere on an empty tank. Similarly, you can't run on gas tainted by water. You will eventually falter and stall, placing you right back where you used to be. Yes, purpose and passion go hand in hand.

Now for the *10 powerful ways to discover true inner peace and happiness:*

STEP 1: EMBRACE CHANGE

Did you know that the average person hates change? In fact, they spend their lives trying to build cocoons to keep change at bay. Little do they know that, like the butterfly, we are a chrysalis that is turned into a human version of the butterfly by the pressure of change. If, in your life, you are receiving the same results, you must change what you are doing. Then and only then will you receive a different result. Knowing this, shouldn't we learn to embrace change? Get serious about it! Determine what your natural gifts and talents are. This list will be different than the one you made regarding your strengths. This list is about the thing(s) you know, without a doubt, that you are better at than anyone else. In fact it's probably the one single and natural thing you dream about spending your life doing. (Your true Passion).

How do you begin working on using the strengths and talents you've found to create positive changes in your life? The answer is, become conscious of the choices you make on a moment-to-moment basis. Create awareness of what it is you are thinking, saying and doing throughout your day. Then begin to make these choices on purpose and with passion.

Part of making positive change in your life is identifying your dreams. Your dreams will probably rotate around those gifts or talents you discovered a few steps back. For example, somewhere within that dream vacation is also a dream of how you came to be there. What is your dream job? Why? How can you achieve it? I'll tell you how ….

Once you've clearly identified your dreams, you need to understand that turning them into reality is all about goal setting. It requires that you reverse engineer those big dreams, breaking them down until you arrive at some task you can do today and in the days to come.

Stay disciplined and focused. Once you begin setting daily goals it's very important that you stay disciplined. No weekdays off or early check-outs for you. True goal-setting requires that you spend your day focused on each goal you apply yourself to—one at a time, hour by hour and day by day—until you reach that far away dream which can create and inner peace and true happiness.

STEP 2. FIND PURPOSE AND PASSION

Self-empowerment is the actuation of the self through minute-to-minute choices. These are choices made on purpose, with real focus and passion. It's the result of knowing your strength and your dreams and having a plan, through goal-setting, to use those strengths to get there.

However, all these changes can increase your stress levels. Happily, the way to decrease stress is to take the task at the top of your prioritized list of goals and put all your focus on it, never thinking of any of the other tasks on your list until you have finished the one you are currently working on—even if you don't finish your list of daily goals. In such a case they just get added to the next day's list. Why does this work? It works because it eliminates worry (most likely one of your biggest stressors). It will also let you get more done than any other system you might happen to try.

I'll tell you a secret. The system of goal-setting I've been talking about will create a new zest for life in you, and it will leave you happier. Why? You'll have virtually eliminated worry in your life. Secondly, our minds are goal-oriented machines. By creating a focused plan, you'll be tapping into that problem-solving aspect of your mind, and it will leave you satisfied at the end of each day. A person who is satisfied with where they are in life and with whatever they have will generally be happier.

Lifestyle change, which is huge and what most individuals desire, will come as you change the decisions you make throughout the day. Make the conscious choice to make positive decisions leading to your goals. Make an extra sale a week, 50 more telephone calls per week, or take on more responsibility at work—all these changes tend to lead to lifestyle changes. So can your daily decisions: the choice to not go for a coffee break at the local café puts more money in your pocket every day; the simple choice to smile in the moment can bring all sorts of changes to your life as you meet new people and enamour the ones you know. The list is endless. Change your moment-to-moment choices and watch your life alter before your eyes.

As you become a more confident decision-maker and an even more stellar goal-setter, you'll undoubtedly notice that your personal confidence will grow exponentially. There's something about making the right choices and doing the right things (for you) that boosts people's confidence immensely.

And ... you may never work again. This point may seem silly to you, but it holds a kernel of truth. When you begin to act on purpose, pursuing goals designed to bring you your greatest dreams, you'll find that you're no longer working but rather you're having fun and experiencing happiness. You'll be filled with a passion for action. No longer will problems plague you, because you'll know that each problem solved takes you a step closer to the fulfilment of your daily goals and your ultimate dreams.

STEP 3. SEVERAL INTERTWINED METHODS FOR OBTAINING INNER PEACE

One way to obtain inner peace is to go in deep with meditation. There are many different forms of meditation, and it's beyond the scope of this piece to point you in a specific direction. Suffice it to say that meditation serves two purposes: 1) to clear the mind and 2) to create an intense feeling of focus and well-being. By going deep into a meditative state you can face whatever it is that lies before you with a renewed sense of passion and clarity of thought. Sounds good doesn't it?

Joining up and networking with individuals who are on a "passion" quest for the gift or talent that will light a fire beneath them like never before is heady stuff and very important. You must surround yourself with "like" minded individuals. These are people who are excited by the prospect of finally discovering and doing what they were born to do. They're a special club of people who are passionately working on achieving their dreams. And that excitement will rub off on you. I am personally involved with a Success Training Company called PEAK POTENTIALS. If you would personally like to take your life to the next level, I recommend you attend their self-development seminar. It's a true life-changing event. You may register at: http://lifepurposeandpassionbook.com/ -- a great group of people to rub shoulders with! You've got to know this will lead to greater inner peace.

Fasting is a biblical way to truly humble yourself in the sight of God (Psalm 35:13; Ezra 8:21). King David said, "I humble myself through fasting."

Fasting can transform your prayer life into a richer and more personal experience. Fasting can also result in a dynamic personal revival in your own life and can make you a channel of revival to others.[1] It most definitely leads to inner peace.

And finally, self-reflection, like fasting, can clear your mind. Serious thought about one's character, actions, and motives can bring a sense of cohesiveness that can't help but create a greater sense of peace.

STEP 4. DISCOVER YOUR LIFE PURPOSE

Many people never discover their "life purpose." They get caught up in earning a living, raising a family and a thousand other different things. They might play wistfully with a hobby they love or they might daydream about doing something they secretly think would bring them the true contentment they desire. But they never quite reach the point where they make the jump to living their dreams.

The truth of the matter is that *Success is ... taking action*. One must become actively aware of what it is that they were put on this earth to do. You know what this is. It's that secret dream you hardly dare to dream of. Or it's something people have always said you were born to do. Whatever your gift or talent is, deep down you know it. You just need to bring it to the forefront of your mind, you need to seek true awareness. Next comes action. The average person never takes enough small steps to create the momentum needed to move forward into the life of their dreams. Success is ... taking action. Break your dreams down into ever smaller tasks until you reach the point where you have a list of things you can do now—today. Act on them.

[1]http://www.cru.org/train-and-grow/devotional-life/personal-guide-to-fasting.2.html

Take the thousand baby steps that will add up to massive action. Begin right now. The number of people who begin the journey to their dreams but never get there are countless. It's not their fault. They never knew that they had to carefully analyze their actions. A ship gets to its destination by making the minute-to-minute analysis of its position and then making course adjustments necessary to stay moving in the direction of the targeted port of call. Do not try to "eat" the whole elephant. Focus and take small steps to reach the bigger goal. Take realistic steps to reach your goals and obtain your dreams because, when you make unrealistic goals, you set yourself up for frustration and ultimately failure. People must chase their dreams in the same way. We must constantly adjust what we do to make sure we stay on the right path.

You might think this path will be too stressful. And stress can kill. Everyone knows that. Well, if you don't want stress then you must first accept that happiness, joy, contentment and beauty are the natural order of things. Did you know that 47% of all cancer cases is due to "pent up anger and resentment? Strive for continued happiness. It may be a stretch at first, because I can almost guarantee you don't have these things in your daily life. It's not your fault. Chances are no one ever taught you how to consciously focus on bringing them into your daily life. That's right: the key to removing stress from your life is to purposely bring happiness, joy, contentment and beauty into your life by making the right choices on a minute-to-minute basis. It's that simple and that difficult. But you can do it. I know you can.

You really must choose the environments mentioned above. Toxic environments kill everything in their path. You must choose to live differently, every minute of your life. And you can't expect to be valued if you don't, first, value yourself. Change your thinking and your actions will change, and people will sense it. They will look at you differently. Because we are, most definitely what we think. The Process of Manifestation is: Thoughts lead to Feelings.

Feelings lead to Actions. Actions lead to Results. Let's get Positive RESULTS in our lives!! Your inner thoughts will determine your outer world!

STEP 5. LEARN TO THINK POSITIVELY

Many people think that positive thinking implies seeing the world through rose-colored lenses, and ignoring or glossing over the negative aspects of life. You know—the glass is half full instead of half empty. However, positive thinking actually means approaching life's challenges with a positive outlook. It does not necessarily mean avoiding or ignoring the bad things; instead, it involves making the most of potentially bad situations, trying to see the best in other people, and viewing yourself and your abilities in a positive light. Such habits reduce stress and increase your level of contentment and happiness.

Why is positive thinking contagious? This is what I call a "no brainer." Who would you rather hang out with: the guy who is always the life of the party or the grumpy guy in the next cubicle at work? The choice is obvious, right? But why is it obvious? It's obvious because the guy who's the life of the party makes you feel good—about the party and about yourself. And therein lies the key. If you alter how you view yourself and your abilities, other people will alter their behaviours regarding you. Call it the psychology of the masses or some other technical term: it doesn't change the fact that, in general, people respond to us based on how we see ourselves.

How can you turn negative thinking into positive thinking? Positive thinking must be made a habit for it to work. That means you must be willing to consciously choose your thoughts or your response to what is going on in your life from a minute-to-minute standpoint, until the process becomes second nature. This takes commitment and hard work, something most people aren't going to do for a process they don't even understand. But you now understand, don't you?

An example of positive thinking: "The history of the baby frog.......

Once upon a time there was a bunch of baby frogs....
... participating in a competition. The target was to get to the top of a high tower. A crowd of people had gathered to observe the race and encourage the participants.....

The start shot rang out.......
Quite honestly:
None of the onlookers believed that the baby frogs could actually accomplish getting to the top of the tower.
They said things like: "Ah, it's too difficult!!!
They'll never reach the top."
or: "Not a chance... the tower is too high!"
One by one some of the baby frogs fell off...
...Except those who quickly climbed higher and higher..
The crowd kept on yelling:
"It's too difficult. Nobody is going to make it!" More baby frogs became tired and gave up...
...But one kept going higher and higher.....
He was not giving up!

At the end everybody had given up, except the one determined to reach the top! All the other participants naturally wanted to know how he had managed to do what none of the others had been able to do!

One competitor asked the winner, what was his secret?

The truth was.......

The winner was deaf!!!!

The lesson to be learned:

Don't ever listen to people who are negative and pessimistic...

...they will deprive you of your loveliest dreams and wishes you carry in your heart! Always be aware of the power of words, as everything you hear and read will interfere with your actions!

Therefore:

Always stay...

POSITIVE!

And most of all:

Turn a deaf ear when people tell you that you cannot achieve your dreams!

Always believe:

You can make it! Stay Positive!!!

STEP 6. ELIMINATE NEGATIVITY

Until you've become strong enough to be able to ward off the negativity in situations it would be a great idea to avoid watching the news. It might even be good to avoid television altogether. Why? Because there's so much that is negative or that will counter your attempts to live a contented and happy lifestyle that it could severely hamper your efforts.

Just to make a point. I turned on the television last night when I got home, and set about having a relaxing evening. There were at least six channels that were talking about current terrorism threats and many other channels were carrying shows full of violence and bloodshed. Tell me how that works to help you change your mindset in a positive way? I'm not saying not to watch television, but be very careful what you put into your psyche.

What was said previously goes double for negative environments. If a situation truly is negative, how do you expect to truthfully change your thoughts about it? You can do it, but you'll most likely be kidding yourself. The way to stay positive, contented and happy is to make certain your day is filled with light and beauty, not darkness and ugliness. Make sense?

Adopt healthy eating habits. Is thinking about having a hamburger and French fries for lunch really bad thinking? It is if you're overweight and your goal is to lose that weight. To adopt healthy eating habits (and this goes for anyone, not just the overweight), one must make those moment-to-moment positive choices we've been talking about. The choice to choose a salad over a hamburger and fries is simple—if you are acting on "purpose."

Focus on the "whats" not the "what ifs." What can I do about my current situation to make it a positive and joyful experience? What if this wasn't happening to me? What if I just skipped out? What if I made the effort to enjoy myself? Which of these questions will make certain my thoughts and actions are going to ensure the best possible experience? If you chose question the first one, then you're beginning to get the hang of "positive thinking." Do not look at opportunities and situations in life and say, "I'll believe it when I see it". You will miss opportunities over and over again. It's the exact opposite, YOU WILL SEE IT WHEN YOU BELIEVE IT" Have Faith! Just because you do not see the seeds growing, doesn't mean, they are not growing. Please refer to the story of the Chinese Bamboo Tree—the story of patience.

What do you love? What do you love to do? I'm not just talking about work here. What leisure activities do you love? What can you do to make sure you build as many of these activities into your days as possible? Remember the goal-setting process? By placing leisure activities on your priority list, you'll be sure to do them when their turn arrives. If I've booked a tee time at my favourite golf course for 2 pm, then I know my workday is going to end at two, and I can prioritize my daily to-do list accordingly, knowing that no matter what happens I will quit working at that time.

Will such practices work every time? Of course not. Life is full of problems and obstacles. But I can guarantee that such habits will bring more pleasure and inner peace into your life than any other method I know of.

STEP 7. DEVELOP YOUR "SELF"

The threat to your continued self-development is inaction. Regardless of the reason or excuse, you can't change anything about your life unless you take purposeful, massive action. Those countless moment-to-moment choices that lead to action of unimaginable proportions must be made on purpose and with specific results in mind. Failure to do this consistently is the one major threat to the achievement of anything you want—include self-development. Best Selling Author T. Harv Eker was quoted saying, "Rich Minded People continue to learn and Grow and Poor "minded" and Middle Class people think that they already know." It's key to invest in your continuous self-development.

Find a life coach. Why do you need a life coach? A person who has already done the things you want to do can guide you past the many pitfalls that lie before you. She can also ensure that you make the right moment-to-moment decisions. She's been there, remember? A successful life coach can shorten your journey by years. Isn't that worth the investment of money and effort? I think it is.

Associate with like minds. People have the ability to affect others through changes in their mindset and their actions. Imagine what could happen if like-minded people came together. The effect could be explosive. I know for a fact that two like-minded people can increase their success exponentially. It's like they form a third mind, a "mastermind," that lifts them up and carries them forward. The effect increases as you add more people to your group. You can even have more than one mastermind group. Some will focus on personal development, some on work and some on investing. You can have a mastermind group for just about any aspect of your life. Anytime two or more like-minded people get together great things can happen.

Read self-help books. Again, you can benefit from those who have gone before you. There are thousands of self-help books out there. And they cover just about any subject you can imagine. Invest in them. There isn't any rule that says your mentor must be a live person. Books can and do teach people how to attain their goals in life.

Enrol in self-development programs. Dale Carnegie, perhaps the greatest motivator ever, taught many, many thousands of people how to achieve their dreams. His books touched many others. His speaking courses were genius in motion. Enrolling in similar courses can give each of us the spark to move forward, to take action with a purpose. You don't have to do this thing alone. Find a program to help you along.

Everything that has been laid down in this outline could be considered the process by which you can change your character and/or your abilities for the better. Don't you think that such positive changes would make you happier and more at peace with yourself? All that remains is for you to take action.

STEP 8. LEARN THE LAW OF ATTRACTION

The law of attraction is the name given to the term that "like attracts like" and that by focusing on positive or negative thoughts, one can bring about positive or negative results. This belief is based upon the idea that people and their thoughts are both made from "pure energy" and the belief that like energy attracts like energy. One example used by a proponent of the law of attraction is that if a person opened an envelope expecting to see a bill, then the law of attraction would "confirm" those thoughts and contain a bill when opened. A person who decided to instead expect a cheque might, under the same law, find a cheque instead of a bill. Although there are some cases where positive or negative attitudes can produce corresponding results, there is no scientific basis to the law of attraction.

How to use the Law of Attraction and how it may assist you: "The one who speaks most about illness has illness. The one who speaks about prosperity has prosperity," Esther and Jerry Hicks write. "You attract all of it." By focusing on something, you make it happen. And oh how true this is. In life focus can be everything. Think about something long enough and hard enough and you're sure to become attuned to actions that can make it happen. The intense focus will also increase the chances that you will act on your thoughts when the opportunity presents itself.

It's very easy for people who know this secret to believe that like attracts like, but I caution against that belief. What is actually happening is you are becoming more alert to and more ready to take the actions that will lead to whatever it is you want. Make enough such choices and you are almost certain to arrive at your destination. And it can really feel like magic!

Successful people know many of the things I've been writing about. They know that if they put themselves out there they will eventually bump into something like they are looking for, whether that's a person, a place, or a thing. It's all about focus and the choices that result.

The old adages are that we reap what we sow, that what goes around comes around and that what we give so shall we receive. The whole point is that our focus/choice combination works every way. Put your focus on giving something different to your community or to your family and you will tend to make choices that will reflect that change in thinking. The changes will be noticed by others, who you can be certain will eventually return the favour however they can. It's a great way to live and you can reap rewards beyond your imagination.

STEP 9. TAKE YOUR QUALITY OF LIFE TO THE NEXT LEVEL

There is nothing so strong and so life-affirming as love. Felice Leonardo "Leo" Buscaglia PhD (March 31, 1924 – June 12, 1998), also known as "Dr. Love," was an American author and motivational speaker, and a professor in the Department of Special Education at the University of Southern California. He believed that, the more you love, the greater becomes your capacity for love, a rather contrary vision of what love is like. This was a view of love as having the infinite power to change us and those around us. In fact he said as much in the following quote: *Too often we underestimate the power of a touch, a smile, a kind word, a listening ear, an honest compliment, or the smallest act of caring, all of which have the potential to turn life around.* – Leo Buscaglia

I could go a step further and say that the greatest phenomenon in the universe is the concept of love. Many see God as love. A fact I know is that the more you give love, the more you tend to receive, whether you're thinking of God or yourself or another. Yes, self-love is important. We can only love our God or our spouse or anyone else as much as we love ourselves. How can it be any different? We can only give what we have and what we know.

This also goes for the intensity of our love. It is our deep belief and our intensity that gives us the power to affect others. For this reason it is a worthwhile exercise to practice intensity of love.

I also admonish you to give as you hope to receive. We have all heard this platitude. It has lost what power it might ever have had. But this does not diminish the truth. If you are willing to sacrifice to give to another or to your community, then you fundamentally change yourself. You become more willing to help, to put yourself out there. People will remember this. So, when the time comes when you are in need, as we all are at some point in life, you'll find that all your sacrifices will be remembered and returned tenfold. It may not be in the way you expect, but it will happen. There's too much anecdotal evidence to believe otherwise.

And as I close, love once again comes into play. Open your heart to the universe and it will fill you up. Give all this back and you will feel as you have never felt before. Some call it a religious conversion, others refer to it as enlightenment; still others speak of a sense of peace and happiness. The bottom line is that you can't love too much. It's impossible. Love can't be used up, so don't be afraid to reach out (take action) for what is waiting for you. You won't regret it.

STEP 10: MORE WAYS TO FIND TRUE INNER PEACE

Apologize and Forgive – When a person apologizes for a wrong he's done or forgives a wrong done unto her an amazing thing happens. All the negative thoughts and emotions you were harbouring simply melt away. You may want to know why this is the case. The answer is incredibly simple: you change your focus. Your moment-to-moment thoughts and actions turn away from what was bothering you and suddenly things are new again.

Relax – Inner peace is a state created by you. Taking time out of your busy day to just relax and allow your mind to drift away to your favourite destinations is a good place to start.

Be Grateful – Happiness and contentment come from being grateful for what you already have. Take your focus and place it on thoughts and actions that indicate to you that you are, indeed, grateful.

Go outdoors – Nature is the great healing balm. A walk in the forest, a stroll through your garden, a ride on your bike or any other outside activity that gets your body moving and breathing in fresh air can't help but improve your disposition.

Go Inside Yourself – The best way I know to go inside myself is meditation, which is the practicing of certain techniques that allow you to clear your mind, heighten your focus and then point your mind in the direction you wish to go.

Know When to Stand Firm – Inner peace is sometimes reached by facing down a problem, whether that be an intense short-term task or a longer-term worry. Face down your problems, find the best way to deal with them, do those things and then forget about them. Inner peace will be yours.

Learn the Power of Surrender – When people talk about surrendering they're usually talking about God. There's something amazingly powerful about giving up yourself and your problems to the holy spirit. I think the largest part of this is that you are giving up all your worries. Joe Tye (CEO and Head Coach of Values Coach Inc., which provides consulting, training and coaching on values-based life and leadership skills.) once said "Worry is ingratitude to God in advance." Think about that for a moment!

Be the Love You Want to Feel – If you want to feel loved, then you must not only love yourself but demonstrate your love for others. It's a risky thing to do—putting yourself out there like that—but you already know that we reap what we sow.

Be of Service – Strange things (good things) happen when you give of yourself to your community, the first of these being a sense of belonging, which goes a long way to creating inner peace.

Be Here Now – And, finally, making the choice to be in the moment, to enjoy each and every one we have during our time on earth, creates such a sense of joy that one soon relaxes and finds a sense of inner peace. Try it, you'll see.[2]

---

[2]http://www.thebridgemaker.com/10-paths-to-true-happiness/

Break Through Your Barriers & Live Your Dreams

Sandra Westland

Every woman deserves to feel powerful and successful, and the opportunity to do so stands right before her. She doesn't have to be a warrior to smite every dragon or burn down every obstacle that stands in her way. She simply needs to connect with and be her real, authentic self. So her journey to success begins by standing still, by being curious about the world of potential that exists within her and in front of her, and by understanding her inner world in order to ignite change in her outer one towards her success.

But, what stops her from becoming the author of her own life, from being all she can be? The glass ceiling, the unofficial barrier that prevents women from rising up to executive positions or from running their successful businesses, does still exist. Yet, in my twenty-five years of education, hypno-psychotherapy and peak performance training, I see, more significantly, an individual's own inner glass ceiling capping and limiting the success in life that is there for the taking.

To be a woman is to be extraordinary. We all have it within us to move beyond an ordinary life and its everyday limitations to embrace our desires and possibilities, harness our untold natural potential and live the life we are meant to live —a life of personal freedom in which we simply are our natural, awesome selves. Your power is switched on when you embrace, embody, express and enjoy being a woman. Your energy is released when you learn to live truly in your own skin. I love being a woman, and I love continuing to find out just what that is like for me.

This is a journey of discovering your place in life as a woman and as a woman in business, a voyage into your inner mind's processing and the terrain of your inner world, deeper than your conscious mind can be aware of. It is an expedition through self-alignment, forming the detail of your desired outcomes, shaping your life to fit with your passions, sourcing the energy that drives you, thus smashing your glass ceiling and allowing your transformation to unfold. Just as I experienced my own first steps, I want you also to stride out along this path and the journey of becoming your potential. The message I write within the pages of *Smashing Your Glass Ceiling* takes you through this fascinating journey where "Wow, I didn't realize that" and "No wonder I wasn't getting to where I wanted to" are familiar insights.

HOW DOES IT ALL WORK?

The tools you will need for such a journey of self-discovery are drawn from Neuro-Linguistic Programming (NLP), guided imagery, and a gentle questing into uncovering your own uniqueness and meaning in life. In blending these time-tested methods into one programme, it's possible to break through all that's holding you back in life.

From my own personal experience as a woman and as a psychotherapist and trainer, I've found that one of the most powerful tools we naturally have and need to embrace first is the power of imagination; even if you think you have one or not, you really do have an amazing, creative imagination. It just may need awakening and a little encouraging. I would love to show you just how powerful your imagination can be and how crucial it is to connect with you and be your own woman. In beginning this imaginative journey, you are sparking off a chain of events that produce fundamental changes in your physical body, starting with the neurological processes that will link to your biology and produce within you "decision states" leading to the different outcomes that you want, easily and naturally. Imagine the decisions that you can make or the actions that you can take when you are feeling confident, in balance and aligned to your vision, compared to the choices that you opt for when you are upset, anxious, depressed and out of sync with yourself.

By guiding your imagination, you can form an internal vision in which you are taking the right path for you to succeed in your life, and then formulate just what that is. As you immerse yourself in the excitement and the thrill of being on the right road to greatness, you tap into the inner confidence and self-reliance, inner freedom and success awareness that generate your momentum to smashing your glass ceiling. The power is always within you. It's just a case of summoning and connecting with it.

Imagine also gaining new understanding into how you process information from your "now" experiences, how you view the world, how you communicate with others and how they communicate with you. Imagine how much easier your life would be. You can learn how to recognize ways of processing external data and how, by modifying your communication in a way that makes sense to others, your relationships become infinitely warmer, richer and more connected.

Think about meeting me in the flesh for the first time, already knowing how my inner world works. Wouldn't it be good to know I'm an auditory person? Why? Well, my world is very much filtered through sounds. I will be finely tuned into noise … all noise. I will get distracted with too much of it, and I will recognize very slight changes in your voice, tone and pitch. So I will hear a hint of doubt or an emotion rising from within you just by hearing your voice. If you speak too slowly or very loudly, this will create a dissonance within me. If you use language that talks about "viewing something" or "seeing what you mean" or "having a handle on this or that" instead of "sounds like" or "listen to", I will feel a mismatch between us. Don't click your pen or tap it on the table if you want me to be relaxed! It's only a slight inner discomfort, but it undeniably shapes how I experience you and your communication. Upon our meeting, if you appreciate my world and I appreciate yours, we will hit it off with ease. I will look to communicate to you through your world, which may be visual, auditory, kinesthetic or auditory digital, all very different ways of experiencing and processing, and you can do the same for me.

GETTING TO KNOW YOUR GLASS CEILING

Your internal glass ceiling may have been created from prejudgments, prejudices, cultural and social attitudes that operate deep within the unconscious, taken in when young. So, it's crucial to find these out and know how they work for you, to understand the inner conflicts that are holding you back and what they mean. In speaking with a senior executive upon her reading *Smashing Your Glass Ceiling*, she'd suddenly become aware of how she was dressing like a man for her banking boardroom meetings. It wasn't her at all, but after further exploration, she realized she had unconsciously thought it would help men relate to her and allow her to be "taken seriously". She was shocked at how unconscious this had been, but she was relieved to learn it and is now enjoying the fun of finding out who she is as a woman in business and what clothes this exploration leads her to wearing. It is only by excavating these unconscious gender biases and other judgments that contribute towards making your own ceiling that you can reveal your real, natural self to yourself and the world. In understanding yourself more and knowing just who you are and how you are in the world, you become free to choose how to respond to situations and to people, and then you really begin to own your own life.

I am wondering just what you are thinking, having read these thousand plus words. Is this possible for you or is your glass ceiling giving you bother, preventing you from imagining and thinking of all that you can be? What does your ceiling hold and what is it whispering to you right now? What is your "default" setting?

Are you someone who assumes you won't find a car parking space and prove yourself right, or do you simply know that it doesn't matter where you park and thus usually find one just when and where you need it? Is a potential redundancy at work a chance to do something different, or a terrible catastrophe that you will never escape? Your attitudes play a massive part in your life experiences, and to how much you can grow. Zig Ziglar's famous saying "Your attitude determines your altitude" is so true. So, how do your attitudes determine how successful you can be?

I have lived and refined through my own personal journey a framework of all the things that are crucial to help you aspire to be. Let's make a start right now, something to get you thinking. Let's peek into those achieving just what you want and begin to emulate some of what they do and how they are. It's as good a place as any to start!

In NLP terms, this is called "modeling". In modeling the behaviors and habits of successful people, we're seeking to learn from successful businesswomen and successful women just what it is that they do, and what it is that they have that makes them successful; not to become them, but to incorporate their winning behaviours into our repertoire, choosing those which are congruent with us and amplifying them. I often explore other women that I admire and am drawn to. In carefully watching what they do and exploring this within my own life, in my way, I can open up to further resources that I naturally have, but have yet to connect with. In Sue Knight's' words, "If you spot it, you've got it." (NLP at Work, 2013)

Now to stoke up those neurological pathways as we vamp it up a little more and transport you forward into your own fabulous future. Familiarize yourself with the state of being successful with no glass ceiling, as if you've already accomplished that level of success, a dress rehearsal if you like. Put on the mantle of success and ask yourself how and what do you feel, how would your day evolve, what can you do now that you couldn't do before. How would others perceive you? Get your brain to make it a done deal so that it can look for it, search it out and create it. This is the self-fulfilling prophecy at its most positive, potent and powerful.

Anticipate now becoming friendly and familiar with a future you who has everything you need and want and to be able to use the guidance of that future you – the answers may very well surprise you. My future self enlightened me as to my fear of success! This helped me find my inner glass ceiling and the meaning of it all, so I could smash it and really begin to find out just what I could do and what was possible in life. I believe that to guide others you have to have lived the journey yourself, and so my own personal journey has and is this path too, encompassing where I am finding myself ... as a woman, an educator, therapist and businesswoman. This is a journey I don't ever intend to stop.

PEELING BACK THE ONION

There is so much more to explore! As humans, we've infinite depths, so exploring your inner beliefs, your values and mission is crucial for success. It's the peeling back of the onion, layer by layer (corny, I know), but I assure you that the exploration, while deep, is richly rewarding. Wouldn't you rather know what's holding you back and why you may feel frustrated with yourself? I know I would. I simply want to make the most of my time on this earth and experience it as much as possible. Life is to be lived and not simply endured and got through.

Excavate your inner beliefs, isolate the limiting ones that have held you back, and then you will easily and naturally begin to fly! Once figured out, you become empowered as you re-think and re-frame beliefs into being resourceful, productive and desirable, and turn them into second nature.

Let's go one deeper. Do you know just what it is that you value, all those things that are really important to you? Are they aligned with your life? These are your GPS, and if you're frustrated, feel trapped in the mundane of life or have unwanted physical/emotional symptoms, then value fine-tuning is needed for you to move forward in the direction that you want to go. Let's not be sidetracked by detours, road closures and an unclear destination. Being authentic and all that you are needs you to know what you value so that you're able to craft your mission for the ultimate alignment. In *Smashing Your Glass Ceiling* or my Success workshops , you will not short-change yourself here. I will journey with you, helping you along the way through a process of simple, yet profoundly powerful steps.

When you are fully aligned, there will be no holding you back. You'll meet the right person at the right time, and you'll have the right skills to achieve your goals. Everything will fall into place like a jigsaw puzzle, and you'll have "the strength, the patience, and the passion to reach for the stars", to borrow the words of a courageously inspiring woman, Harriet Tubman.

LOADING UP ON INTERNAL RESOURCES

It's not all plain sailing, and you *will* be derailed by the unexpected, but what makes someone a success is their ability to keep going, even when challenged. So, one of the final steps in the Programme is to load you up with the internal resources to get you through when things get sticky, and when, quite frankly, you wonder why you bother. NLP strategies reprogram how we react and respond to such times, making a monumental difference to how you experience your life. If you're feeling down on yourself, I will show you that you can change your physiology. If you're getting increasingly anxious about an upcoming meeting, you can change your self-talk, the inner conversation you're having with yourself, to something more upbeat, more encouraging and more positive.

Powerful NLP strategies are there for you to use at any time and in any situation. Your life will be richer and filled with more options when you are able to redirect your thinking and focus, stay resourceful in stressful situations, and generate behaviors and outcomes that are positive for you and your life.

Finally, if this chapter has inspired you to delve deeper into Smashing your Glass Ceiling, the book comes with a number of bonuses, some of which can be downloaded from my website, www.SmashingYourGlassCeiling.com for you to enjoy absolutely free. So, get started now and embrace the fact that you are an extraordinary woman.

TAKING THE FIRST STEP

All of us have to start somewhere. I did when I was thirty-four, when I found myself looking at twenty-six more years before retirement, counting the years and the days till the next school holiday. Not how I imagined my life would be.

By becoming curious, asking questions of myself and tapping into effective life-changing techniques that opened me up to the power and potential of the mind, I'm on a fascinating journey. I'm continuing to smash my own internal glass ceiling, and am living out my passion to enhance the lives of other women. I am certainly not "sorted out", nor have I "self-actualized" and not every day is "grrreat", but I know that every day is an adventure with the chance to grow further and find out more about just what is possible.

The more women I meet and work with, the more I learn and the more I gather evidence to support my belief that, as women, we owe it to ourselves to be extraordinary. This is my invitation to you to take the first steps with me on your own journey of becoming all you wish to be.

Sandra Westland is an experienced educator, therapist and successful businesswoman who helps others to find their passion and fulfil their dreams. She has a Master's degree in Existential Psychotherapy, an Education Honours degree, and is a practicing Advanced Hypnotherapist and NLP practitioner. Her doctoral thesis explores women and their relationship with their bodies. She is the author of Smash Your Glass Ceiling and co-author of Thinking Therapeutically.

Sandra is a Director of the Contemporary College of Therapeutic Studies, where she trains people at life changing junctures to be aspiring therapists, so they too can enjoy the enriching privilege of helping others to find their path in life. She is also a co-founder of Self Help School™, which provides psycho-education for the public and is an international speaker on the power of the mind for change.

Create the Life of Your Dreams

The Savvy Investor's Ultimate Guide to Wholesaling Real Estate

DEXTER MONTGOMERY & PAMELA MONTGOMERY

Many people look to real estate investment as an enjoyable, flexible, and dependable way to generate income. Whether that means supplementing a day job or completely transforming the way you spend your time and fund your lifestyle, you might be one of these people. Even in a changing housing market, real estate continues to represent an essential part of the economy – neighborhoods transition, young people grow up, properties continue to be bought and sold; great deals are always out there.

The allures of investing in real estate are many – being your own boss, making your own hours, earning more than you ever have before, setting your own financial goals and having the means to meet them – but, while it can be extremely rewarding, entering into real estate can also be very challenging.

The inexperienced will not know the many ins and outs of buying, selling, renting, and rehabbing properties: everything from the appropriate lingo (a must if you want to be taken seriously) to housing market trends and the function of different specialists with whom you must work to be successful. That doesn't even include general entrepreneurial skills like setting goals and educating yourself; these things are absolutely essential to success in real estate investment as well.

As in many other fields, experience can be invaluable in investment, but knowing the lay of the land before you ever get your feet wet is essential. The process of trial and error is not so desirable when an "error" means losing a substantial portion of a large amount of money you have invested.

If you are serious about establishing a career or side-career in real estate investment, you will most certainly make mistakes and experience hardships along the way and, if you are patient and resilient, you will learn from them. However, you have to put the time and effort in before you get involved to ensure that you know what you're doing.

Real estate coaches and seminar speakers will often talk about all the mistakes they made when they were starting out. In this field, that means losing money, sometimes a lot of it. Consider yourself lucky to have the option of using their advice and expertise to help you avoid these same mistakes. Some of this information is free, but immersing yourself in the necessary knowledge will require an investment. You must trust that, if you find the right programs, seminars, coaches, books, and other resources, it is worth every penny.

You will not get to where you need to be by reading one chapter on the subject, but it's a great start. If you're serious about pursuing this opportunity that you know can make your life better and help you realize your goals, you will use a resource like this chapter as a diving board into the "deep end," so to speak, where you can really educate and immerse yourself.

FORMS OF REAL ESTATE INVESTMENT

On a basic level, a big part of diving into real estate investment is a decision about what form of investment to pursue. Eventually, as you grow with your business, you might very well want to expand your efforts, trying different types of investments and determining which ones make the most sense for you and for different types of situations. However, when you are just starting, it is important not to overextend yourself. You will do well to focus on only one type of investment.

What really differentiates one kind of real estate investment from another is the "exit strategy" for a given property. If you think of your initial acquisition of the property as your "entrance," and your plans for that property as your "exit," you begin to see that there are many different options. Planning your exit strategy before you acquire a property is essential to understanding how you will profit from the transaction.

These are the most common ways to profit from a real estate investment:

- **Wholesale**: Acquiring a property at a favorable price from a motivated seller and quickly reselling it to a motivated buyer. You might be selling the property to someone who will then pursue one of the following strategies.

- **Rental**: Acquiring a property and holding on to it for the long term, earning profit on it by leasing to a tenant.

- **Rehab**: Also known as "flipping" a property. It's more of a long term project than wholesale buying and selling. Rehabbing involves acquiring a distressed property and fixing it up to bring up its value, then reselling it.

These various forms of investment differ in several ways, from timeline to resources required to marketplace appropriateness, and many more. A certain property may be better suited to one of these investment methods than to the others. Comparing your expected costs to your expected income will help you decide which is most appropriate.

For example, rehabbing a property balances the combined cost of acquiring it and bringing it back to life against what someone will pay you for it once you've done so. Renting is only prudent when you know the income from your tenant will cover your costs – that includes acquiring, holding, and maintaining the property.

If you intend to wholesale a property, you must have a good understanding of how quickly you can expect to sell it, and at what price. Simply holding on to a property will be one of your costs, due to property tax, so how quickly you sell will determine how much you can profit from that sale. Likewise, buying and reselling a property will, of course, only be profitable to you if your sell price is higher than your buy price. Researching comparable sales, both from a timing and a pricing perspective, will help give you a read on this. The better you know the neighborhood you're buying and selling in, the better you can understand what to expect.

Other factors to consider, both when deciding between types of investment and when determining whether or not to buy in at all, include:

- **Financial risk**: How much are you willing to take on?

- **ROI** (Return on Investment): How much money do you expect to make from this deal, and how quickly do you expect to make it?

- **Your time**: How much time will you have to research the deal? How much time will you have to devote to managing/fixing up/appraising/marketing the property?

- **Your effort**: How much effort are you willing to put into the above considerations?

- **Financing**: Where will the money you are investing come from?

WHOLESALING

As discussed above, dipping your toes into the water of real estate development is a great place to start but, if you're serious about pursuing it, you will eventually dive in all the way. The rest of this chapter will discuss in greater detail one specific facet of real estate investment: wholesaling. You'll want to continue to seek out additional resources to get deeper into the others.

Wholesaling is a great entry point because getting into it doesn't require as much money up front as some of the other types of investment do. As mentioned above, a wholesaler is essentially a "middle man" between a motivated buyer and a motivated seller. Let's dig a little deeper into who these people are and how they are relevant to you, the investor.

Motivated Buyers

To those without a lot of real estate experience, the idea of a property buyer might bring to mind a family buying a home, or a business owner buying a commercial space to use as a storefront or office. Images in media or perhaps from personal experience probably bring to mind buyers concerned about location, and looking for a space they will "fall in love with." You might picture a couple that wants space to raise children and access to good schools, or a store owner looking for an area with good visibility and ample room for storage.

Although these kinds of things are important to certain types of real estate deals, they are not so relevant to the wholesaler. The family and the business owner would not be examples of motivated buyers. Rather, a motivated buyer is someone with ready access to cash, looking for a good investment him- or herself. A motivated buyer will "fall in love" with a property if the numbers indicate that it represents a good business deal.

Finding and attracting these motivated buyers becomes much easier when you are offering them an attractive price. This is why understanding the market is so important in a wholesale deal. You have to be sure that, when you buy a property, you will be able to resell it at a price that is low enough to easily and quickly attract motivated buyers and high enough to provide you with a profit.

Offering great deals to motivated buyers – and handling transactions professionally and ethically – will encourage those buyers to come back to you again and again, looking for more opportunities to buy from you. As your business grows, you can begin to put together a database of names and build a network.

In fact, networks of this kind already exist in many forms, and getting access to them is a great first step to finding motivated buyers. Joining a local real estate investment club is one way to meet other investors and begin to build your network. You can also meet investors by attending property auctions. Networking in this way is an invaluable part of getting started in property wholesaling.

Motivated Sellers

Let's talk about the other side of the equation, the motivated seller. Just as a motivated buyer is someone with cash in hand, looking to buy quickly, rather than someone carefully searching for a property to "fall in love with," a motivated seller is not somebody who would like to sell a property, or is maybe considering it, but somebody who has to sell, for one reason or another.

A motivated seller will have a strong reason (usually a financial one) compelling him or her to sell. Falling behind on a mortgage, suffering a personal hardship like divorce or loss of a job, and inheriting an unwanted property are examples. As a wholesaler, you are in a position to solve a problem for a motivated seller. You can take a property off the seller's hands and move it to someone who wants it.

In this way, real estate wholesaling is really a win-win-win situation. The seller gets rid of an unwanted or unsustainable property, the buyer finds a good investment and you, the wholesaler, essentially earn a fee for bringing these two parties together. You might think of this as a sort of "finder's fee."

So how do you find these motivated sellers? There are several different strategies you might consider. These sellers have to know that you are available to provide them with this service, so marketing yourself is essential.

Advertising is an important way to get onto a potential seller's radar, be it through the newspaper, the internet, or even a sign along the road.

You can also proactively look for properties by combing through listings or by driving or walking around in an area and hunting for "For Sale" signs. When physically going around and looking at properties, seek out distressed or vacant homes and "FSBO" (For Sale by Owner) signs. While searching through listings, keep an eye out for expiring listings and those labeled things like "Handyman Special" or "Needs Work".

Here again, networking can come in handy, as working with real estate agents who search the MLS (Multiple Listing Service) can give you access to these types of listings. Another group, sometimes known as "bird dogs," can be a great resource too. Bird dogs are people who pass on good deals to wholesalers, for a fee. As with motivated buyers, if you are respectful and ethical in your dealings with real estate agents and bird dogs, they will want to continue to work with you and bring deals to you.

If you find a property you're interested in, you can send a postcard or a letter to the owners, offering to help solve their problem. If need be, you can find names and addresses in government property tax records.

You may make many, many offers before one is accepted, so patience is incredibly important to finding success in wholesaling. Once you get some momentum behind your business and build your network, you will have more resources for finding good opportunities for investment, but when you dive in you will need the determination to overcome rejection.

KEEP LEARNING!

Now that you know a little bit about investing in real estate, and specifically the strategy of wholesaling, you are in a great position to build on that knowledge. If the financial flexibility and excitement of buying and selling property grabs your interest, you will want to dig much deeper. There are so many resources to seek out, from books to internet forums to seminars to coaches and mentors. Don't cut corners; continue to educate yourself and you'll be in great shape to dive into this exciting field.

A Dream Life for the Asking

TOM BARBER

There is an enchanting transformation that occurs during those fleeting moments between sleeping and waking as you emerge out of a deep, relaxed slumber before the demands of the day come tumbling into your conscious world. It is also a magical moment of pure potentiality that contains seeds of inspiration or a solution to that insolvable problem that has hounded you for days. Just as you're about to reach out for that breakthrough thought (the one that teeters on the edge of your consciousness), the alarm clock rings, your smartphone dings a text message alert, your baby cries or your dog bays for food. You lose that thread of inspiration; it's gone as if it never existed.

Have you experienced those moments when you say, "But I just had it in my head, it was *right* there!" only to realize that creativity has tenuously slipped through your fingers?

What if you were able to access this state of pure potentiality as often as you wanted to, when you wanted to? You may require some expert assistance in the beginning to reprogram your beliefs so that you know it is, indeed, possible. However, once you've exercised your "mental muscles" and familiarised your mind and body often enough to get the process fully, you will be able to tap into this infinite source of creativity, inspiration, solutions and possibility at will. What if you could access this untapped power for health, greater happiness and contentment, and for peak performance and success, as if it were "second nature"? Well, you can.

Hypnosis is the technology I use to usher people into deep trance states where they can connect to their inner power. Coined by James Braid, a 19th century Scottish surgeon, the term hypnosis comes from "Hypnos," the Greek god of sleep. You don't fall asleep during hypnosis, however; instead you enter a state of deep, calm relaxation during which you can work directly with your subconscious, that part of your mind that takes care of everything behind the scenes.

Back to that moment in the morning, when you're woken up by the barking of your dogs. From that point on, your conscious mind takes over; it goes through the checklist of what you've got to do during the day, the meetings you've got to attend, the chat you're going to have with your boss or travel plans you're going to make for your next vacation. It seems as if the conscious mind is calling the shots, but actually the subconscious mind is continually doing all the hard work.

It is the subconscious that keeps the heart beating, and that tells your lungs to keep pumping oxygen, which speeds up the movement of your legs as a car is threatening to run you down while you are crossing the street. When you cut yourself, you don't think logically to yourself, "Okay, time for the blood to clot now and the white cells to come fight off infection!" All these seemingly simple, yet intricate reactions are silently and efficiently orchestrated by the powerful subconscious. Think of it as your life's Control Panel.

The pure power of the subconscious is revealed in fleeting moments all the time, even when you're asleep. We're just not always aware it's happening. When you've had a stroke of inspiration, or the genius of an idea, that moment of "divine aha!" leaps out like a Jack-in-the-box, released into your conscious mind. The latter is often met, however, with the vast amounts of data, external stimuli, emotions and physical experiences that are part of your interaction with the world from moment to moment. The trick is to keep the genius intact and to expand its reality within your conscious world. You can learn how to do that too.

The subconscious is the seat of imagination, impulse, creativity and emotion and is also the storehouse of your memories, which means it's one mighty big reservoir. Tapping into it at will and harnessing its power can be truly awesome.

SO WHAT DOES IT ALL MEAN?

What does all this have to do with hypnosis? How can it reveal to us such inner power? Hypnosis takes you to that relaxed state, where your brain frequency literally slows down. Your subconscious mind can then come to the front of the stage as the headline act and revel in the spotlight. In a hypnotic trance state, you remain alert, but you're incredibly focused, just as if you were fully engaged in a really good book or a compelling movie. You switch off external stimuli and are fully engaged in the world of the book or film as if you were right there, in the story.

Hypnosis gives you the key to open the door to the subconscious, access its amazing wealth of information, creativity and resources. It allows you to "anchor" a positive mindset and feelings to be accessed at any point in the future. In this manner, you gain distinct control of your emotions and can manage your mindset for positive behaviour, essentially creating the outcomes you've only ever dreamed of before.

Let's take an example. Let's say you almost drowned when you were a little kid and have since avoided the water. Now an adult, every time you approach the sea, you have a plunging feeling in your stomach. You feel left out on beach holidays because you're afraid of being too close to the water; you don't even dip a toe in the swimming pool. However, you've fallen in love with a marine biologist and you feel that there's something missing if you can't share the love of being in the water with your new partner. Are you always going to stay on the sidelines, or are you going to engage with life so you can have endless fun and build great memories with the love of your life? Which would you choose?

You've been dominated by fear surrounding the bad experience but, with hypnosis, I can take away the sting of the anxiety and terror, as well as any undesirable thoughts that creep into your mind unwillingly at the sight of the ocean. Then, I can help you replace those unhappy memories with a new, more desirable set of emotions and sensory experiences. I can explore with you any feelings of fun, delight and sharing that you've encountered previously in doing something else, like playing football or cooking with friends, and link those feelings with being in the water. By taking these steps, we would together reprogram your mind-body connection so that it reacts positively to swimming and everything associated with it, such as soaking up the warm sun, feeling the breeze, tasting the salt in the water, thriving in the adventure and, ultimately, enjoying more intimate love!

To ensure you can re-access this desirable state, I use a technique called Clenched Fist Auto Anchoring to make sure that these positive emotions are powerfully stored in your body's memory. By anchoring this sensory experience and all its powerfully positive benefits that are meaningful to *you*, it ensures that you can retrieve or spark happy feelings and sensations around water any time you want, in any situation, at will.

Together, through hypnosis, we will have moved you from a previously inhibiting fear to a pleasurable and fearless sense of freedom and adventure. Your whole world will have just changed immeasurably. This is just one example of how well hypnosis works; it is effective in all situations, from helping you pass your driving exam to overcoming your anxiety around public speaking to surmounting weight problems, habits and low-esteem, to finding your life's purpose and creating great success beyond your wildest dreams.

BELIEVE YOU DESERVE MORE, GET MORE

Hypnotherapy is a powerful technology, and it changes lives. The first step forward begins with *you*.

Ask yourself…
- Do you feel that your life could be better lived?
- Do you long to contribute more positively to your family, your friends, your customers and to the world at large?
- Do you feel frustrated because you don't know which direction to take?

- Are you just plain stuck and unwilling to get out of the hole?
- Do you feel there's a vision inside you waiting to be birthed, but you don't know what it is?

The good news is that you'll never have to live another day feeling "less than" or empty, or thinking you're incompetent, unworthy or undeserving. As long as you believe that positive change is possible, that you deserve more than what you're getting right now and that you are capable of great achievements and deeds, positive change is not only possible, it's yours for the taking. What you need now is *the how*.

Hypnosis addresses that "how," that all-important nourishing factor that creates the changes you desire. It's not "if" you can change, but "how" we are going to do this. In my 20 years of experience as a highly qualified psychotherapist using hypnosis and Neuro-Linguistic Programming (NLP), and through my continuing studying and questing, I've found what I believe to be the essential essence that creates the magical moment of true potential where the hypnotic transformation can effortlessly evolve.

The key lies with the ability of one human being to connect with another as well as being deeply attuned to the knowledge and skills inextricably linked to the hypnotic encounter. This is what allows me to connect to the remarkable depth of experience and human-ness of the person who sits by my side. It's about having a true desire to guide you simply through your journey of change, fully believing you can change, even when, right in that moment, your belief is wavering.

Your connection and trust *will* shape and influence the depth of inner journeying, the quality of your therapist's language *will* impact the speed at which you arrive at your desirable state of being, and his or her ultimate belief and faith that change is yours for the taking will impact your ability to access these positive experiences in the future. This I have seen many, many times.

Within myself, I have uncovered the ability to create deep levels of connection with my clients at lightning fast speed, allowing change to happen seamlessly, where extraordinary shifts are open for those who want to achieve, with definitively measurable results. Through my work with many thousands of clients and students, I have harnessed an ability to quickly "feel" where someone is at, to understand how to navigate around their inner terrain and to engage their trust. This ignites their own belief that they can change and really take back control of their futures. I completely believe that change is yours for the taking if you are doing the asking. It is this belief that shines through and creates formidable levels of expectation. When this is in place, the path to change is fully open to the methods and techniques of *how*.

I've been privileged to share amazing transformations as I've delivered conferences and workshops around the world in places such as Eastern Europe, China, Russia and Mexico, all via an interpreter. It's truly phenomenal to experience the depth of the human connection that comes to the fore when words no longer offer a possible means of instant communication, creating a profound and unforgettably moving experience as inner change unfolds before our very eyes.

Such learning has really equipped me to *know* how to move past the words of a story to the deep, true thoughts and feelings of another human being longing for things to change. No two clients are the same, so there's no cookie-cutter approach, but I believe in some fundamentals to embody, some skills that crucially lead the way alongside the "how" for this particular, unique human being with more potential than he or she yet knows. And that's my wonderful job, my life and my inspiration!

My passion for healing others, and my unwavering exploration into my world as my own journey unfolds, places me in the unique position of travelling the path that will need to be walked for this journey of life to evolve further for you too. I've climbed the mountain before, and I know the track well, so I can guide the people I work with from where they are now to where they want to be. And, if they aren't sure about where that is, I can help them locate just what that destination point is too.

My decision to become a therapist fanned an inner flame, which I hadn't known existed, to learn the art of helping others and changing lives. As I engaged in helping others, I found that I tapped into another joy, learning the depths of myself, discovering my inner undiscovered dimensions, becoming freer and more engaged with life and my healing practices. And so the journey continues to unfold.

LIVING A LIFE TO BE PROUD OF

Those are some of the benefits I would like to pass on to you. You see, there is so much that we can do … and so much that you can do too. You can learn to self-hypnotise for those times when you have no access to a trained therapist, so you can harness your tremendous personal power and live a life of which you are proud.

You might be surprised to discover that you *already* self-hypnotise. We all do. Driving to work and being oblivious of your journey, watching TV and losing track of the plot, finding yourself daydreaming out of the office window. These are all examples of drifting into a state of hypnosis. Imagine learning what you can do with that!

Think about the customs that sports teams go through before a big game – the pre-game rituals and the pep talks that are meant to pump up the team and strike fear in the hearts of the opponents.

In the formidable game of rugby, my all-time passion, the New Zealand All Blacks like to take the temperature up a notch and intimidate the competition by performing the Haka, the traditional Maori dance. It involves loud war cries, heavy pounding of feet, stylised gestures of violence, fierce facial expressions with hanging tongues and glowering stares, all barely feet away from the competing team. Yet, the purpose is not just to frighten off the opposing players; the gestures and stomping are a means of "hypnotising" themselves into states where they are strong, fierce and powerful. It is a means by which they tap into the legendary courage of the Maori warriors of old.

So, a dream life is yours for the asking. If you believe you can have an expanded life with more creativity, more accomplishments, more freedom and more passion, if you believe you can be more aligned, the "how" is right there in your hands. It really is within your reach and your grasp. I invite you to walk the path with me, and would be honoured to be your companion in growth.

Once Tom Barber discovered hypnotherapy, he found himself reinvigorated and re-engaged with life, soon desiring to help others as he was himself helped. He has become a leading Hypnotherapist and Psychotherapist helping people to make changes they so desperately want and can have through hypnosis.

Tom is an international instructor and in-demand Speaker, and is the award winning author of *The Book on Back Pain: The Ultimate Guide to Permanent Relief*, *The Change Sequence*, and Co-author of *Thinking Therapeutically: Hypnotic Skills and Strategies Explored*. Additionally, he is a Director at Contemporary College of Therapeutic Studies UK, where he trains others also wanting to embark on an enriching and fulfilling career in making a difference to others' lives, whilst also co-ordinating SelfHelpSchool™, which provides Self Help through education for the public. Tom, who is known as 'The Changeologist', consults 'leading lights' in the arenas of sport, art and music, as well as the corporate world, all who are committed to inspirational change and growth strategies using the power of the mind. You can contact Tom at Change@TomBarber.co.uk

Awakening Your Healer Within

The Miracle of You

PHILIP YOUNG

In this book you will glean information from "authorities" who offer mind-expanding ideas and concepts that will benefit your entire life and wellbeing. After countless hours of extensive study, thousands of client sessions, and twenty-five years experience, I am excited to be an authority. In my case, the particular subject of expertise is energetic healing and, like the other authorities in this book, I am pleased to share some of this information and knowledge with you. When learned and understood correctly, energetic healing has the ability to uplift, enlighten, and heal either you or a loved one.

To begin, we must define energetic healing. This is a metaphysical healing that takes place beyond the limits and assumptions of physical science known today. In reading this, you will learn how your inner, non-physical energy affects your health and wellbeing, and how this non-physical energy can be harnessed to assist you, sometimes in miraculous ways.

Today, most people see good health as something that is outside of their control, something that they have to fight to maintain. Health is also usually seen as that which is administered to them by outside medical experts and specialists, but there is another approach. What would it be like if, instead of seeking immediate traditional medical assistance, we embraced and recognized the body's own infinite wisdom? Could we then make changes from within? As people are able to open their minds to it, the answer to this question is most emphatically yes. All the wise and experienced physicians I've met with agree that, even with the scientific knowledge that has been gained over the years, we still know very, very little about the complexities of the human body. We are just beginning to scratch the surface of the miracle that we are.

The point of mentioning how little we know is to emphasize that there is another way of being, a way that truly 'does no harm' and is ultimately within your own control and power. If chosen, this is a path that leads to a radiant, healthier, and happier life that will help fill you with greater joy and wonder than ever before experienced.

Let's start with history. In ancient times it was understood that the natural state of human beings was one of vibrant health, and that this vibrant health came from the Self within. As science progressed, facts and data began to take precedence and this inherent knowledge was lost, buried, changed, or distorted. Now, millennia later, these truths are slowly being rediscovered.

I'd like to suggest that the secret of your entire health lies within you, and it is something that you can control with intention. It is something to be conscious of and to take responsibility for. This is a concept seldom taught or understood, which is especially regrettable because it takes so little commitment and discipline. In much the same way as other daily habits become routine, such as brushing your teeth, taking control of your health can be just that easy.

Many people regard themselves as victims or survivors of a disease (dis-ease), and this attitude has been encouraged in various ways in our society. It is a viewpoint that diminishes the Self and gives power to others. As you begin to consider yourself empowered as an active director of your own health, you engage your mind, spirit and body with intent, allowing miraculous changes to occur.

Every moment of every day, millions of cells are being created perfectly within your lungs, your organs, and your blood. All this takes place at the will of non-physical energy and is without any conscious effort on your part. It occurs simply by your inherent desire and intent. This is a monumental clue to the Truth and the beginning of realizing that you already are a miracle! This non-physical energy fills and actually enlivens your cells, tissues, and even your DNA. In fact, it permeates your entire being. Without being too esoteric, think of it as a 'Life Force', one that ultimately gives you Life and also determines your level of health and wellbeing. In circumstances when your health may not be currently optimal, this energy may have been compromised in some way. However, with help, application and some minimal training, it can be redirected to once again be a positive and beneficial resource for your body.

The dilemma that we have in our limited and often blinkered western way of looking at the world is that this non-physical energy has yet to be measured by material instruments. Society as a whole believes that, if something can't be measured, it cannot be. This line of reasoning actually mimics that of well-meaning priests from medieval times, who might have rigorously dismissed the concept of radio waves simply because they did not have the means to measure them at the time. That way of thinking is archaic. Non-physical energies can be perceived by those who are trained and considered to be attuned, open, and intuitively gifted. Moreover, the effects of these energies can be seen and experienced by all, whether or not we are aware of them.

For many years I have had the good fortune to help people experience healings that have been described as miraculous and even impossible. The people who have experienced healing have been able to reach a certain place within them of greater possibility. The process felt so natural, gentle, and effortless for them that they were often not even consciously aware of it taking place. In much the same way that you can use a magnifying glass to ignite kindling or paper, with my assistance people are able to reach a place of perfect health, a place Within that they ordinarily could not reach on their own.

So, how on earth do you reach the place Within that is already perfect? It is similar to tuning in to a radio station. In this case, however, you are tuning in to a subtle part of your Self. Continuing the radio metaphor, you may well experience some static, but if you persist you are able to tune in to that perfect part of you. As you invite the energy to come forth, hold a strong and consistent intent. Don't give up. When people struggle with this, occasionally they'll recall how they were when they were little children: carefree, happy, and hopefully in perfect health. A child's mind is filled with the exact joyfulness, openness and trust you are seeking. By holding onto these memories, the process may be easier.

To tune in to this station, it is also important to maintain a conscious feeling of gratitude for your perfect health in this very moment, regardless of present outward appearances. It's also important to suspend the activities of the intellect and ego and to control the mind chatter. You must move gently and in a state of deep relaxation through your feeling Self and through your loving Heart. By allowing yourself to maintain this thankfulness and gratitude for the miracle that you are, you can continue to fine tune this channel of perfection.

Because the process is unfamiliar, it can seem difficult at first. Most people find it far easier to begin with my help, and they always have beneficial results when they do. This occurs simply by my being fully Present with individuals in each visit with them. I speak with and listen to each person with patience and compassion. Using the vibration of my voice, and the heat and healing touch of my hands both on and around my clients' bodies, I'm able to help them find that place of perfection that's Within.

Over the years, I have found that there are always emotional hurts and concerns (real or imagined) that affect the wellbeing of the individual. Often, there are few if any people who have the time, patience, or compassion, and who are willing to listen to these concerns, much less respond in a supportive and loving way. Many doctors and specialists I meet sadly agree that they only have a few minutes to spend with each patient. Seldom do they learn much about the individual's hopes, past, fears, loves, concerns, personalities, relationships or families. So for them, if that were the case, it just wouldn't be possible to determine how non-physical energies may be of help to those in need.

When I meet clients in need of non-physical healing I allow the vibration of unconditional Love and highest intention to come forth. These energies can be felt as heat in my hands. Sometimes people actually think I have electric heating pads placed on their body. My own body becomes very warm, even hot, as these non-physical energies flow. It is a process of surrendering, of trusting without any ego whatsoever. Something much, much greater is present and in control. Usually this occurs for about an hour and then the energies stop, as the individual is complete. It is much the same way as we stop pouring water into a glass when it is full. No more can be added for the time being.

I feel most blessed to share these deep, sacred insights into the world of each individual. It allows for another aspect of their health, wellbeing and hope to blossom forth and then they feel better. True healing has to consider the totality of the person. It's a matter of body, mind, and spirit.

The following pages chronicle a few of the positive results I've obtained during my many years of practice. These anecdotal accounts demonstrate how real people have experienced wonderful results during healing sessions. Remember, if one man, woman, or child can do it, then so can another! Perhaps you are seeking a remedy at a time when other choices seem dim. If so, it could be that I might be able to help you or a loved one in some way. Whatever the reason, our Hearts and minds have crossed here for a sacred reason. I do hope that you enjoy the material on these pages and that you are inspired to implement the ideas for yourself, or perhaps to share them with others. Within the sanctity and authority of your own Self, take Heart, remain hopeful, and have faith that another way is surely at hand.

BREAST CANCER

"Your breasts are all clear."

Many years ago a dear and beloved friend called one day to say she had breast cancer. Little did I know then that her journey would help me embark on my own journey to becoming a healer.

Trish had been diagnosed with breast cancer and she was dreading the usual medical approach of "cut, poison, and burn" that still today seems to be the one size fits all medical standard. She had been endeavoring to learn as much as possible about her disease, including various alternative ways to treat her condition. She was fearful of chemotherapy's associated toxicity and the side effects that she knew would be so debilitating for her long-term health and wellness. She was open to another approach that was not harmful to her.

After many years of my own esoteric studies and interests, I was now faced with the stark reality of speaking my truth and endeavoring to do something for her or saying nothing while still trying to be supportive. Many of us have often found ourselves in similar situations. It's a matter of walking the talk vs. talking the talk.

I asked Trish if she was willing to try some healing after she had a lumpectomy. She answered yes and was, in fact, willing to try anything that might help. One day we sat down on her cottage lakefront and, to the bemusement of her husband and my wife, began to try a healing process I had read about. I felt certain and hopeful that I could really help her. That day, for about an hour we held the first of several such sessions, not really knowing what to expect, but highly desirous of a good outcome. Although these were just early steps at the time, nonetheless the good outcome arrived! Her breast cancer disappeared completely and to this day, over 20 years later, her breasts are cancer free!

LIFE SENTENCE

"We can't understand it. The tumors are gone."

Several months later I received a phone call from Jillian, a woman referred to me by Trish. Jillian had cancer throughout her body and had been diagnosed as only having a month or two to live. She was told to go home and get her affairs in order. We arranged to meet at her home and we spoke at length about what was going on in her life.

For the first five weeks we gently dealt with some personal issues that she had experienced. On each visit as I spoke with her I laid my hands upon her as she went into a deep guided relaxation. She returned to the hospital for follow up scans and tests, much to the amazement (and even anger, she said) of her medical doctors, as she had defied their diagnosis. Her tumors were either shrinking or had disappeared completely! Over the next several months she and I continued her healing sessions to the point where all tumors were completely gone.

I continued to see Jillian occasionally for over a two-year period. Years later, she eventually passed, but her life and vitality had been extended so much to the everlasting joy of her family, friends and loved ones.

COMA

"Your daughter is going to be in a permanent vegetative state. We are sorry, but there is no hope."

I happened to meet Rita by chance in an office where she was working. Rita told me her daughter Katrina had been struck by a car and had been thrown 70 feet. She had severe head trauma and had been in a coma for several weeks and, at this point, it was expected by the doctors that she would be in a permanent vegetative condition. There was nothing more they could do for her.

When I was a little boy I experienced head trauma and have always felt a deep sense of compassion and empathy for those who have head injuries.

When Rita told me about Katrina, I knew that I had to see her. Out of the blue, I asked Rita if she would be open to that and she said yes.

The next day, walking down the corridors of the hospital, part of me was asking what in the world I was doing there. Part of me wanted to get out of there before I made a complete fool of myself. And yet, another part of me was serene, sure, and calm. I felt like something was guiding me.

Rita was already in Katrina's room and we exchanged a few words. The doctors would not know what I'd be doing, but a couple of the nurses had been informed so that we would not be disturbed quite so much. Seeing Katrina so unresponsive on her bed was quite unsettling. What was I going to say to her? How could this possibly work without a verbal exchange? Without any feedback? With no clues from the eyes? Then I felt a still, calm knowing within me that became my guide. I moved the bed out from the wall, leaned over, and put my hands gently on first Katrina's head, then arm, then hand. Her mom simply looked on, accepting. After about 45 minutes, the healing session seemed to be complete. I really didn't know what to expect. This was new territory for me.

A day later, Rita phoned me to tell me that Katrina had moved her thumb and that the doctors had said this was a reflex. I replied that this is exactly the type of reflex we wanted! A few days later I went back to the hospital and repeated the session, gently touching her arm, her heart, as well as her head. Rita phoned again with good news; this time that Katrina had moved her arm. When I checked my messages a couple of days later I heard one from Rita. Katrina had spoken! I was so overjoyed to hear that and tears ran down my face. It was Christmas Day – what a gift! I saw Katrina several more times and I'm so thrilled that she made a full and quite miraculous recovery.

BRAIN BLOOD VESSEL PROBLEMS (AVM)

"I could drop dead at any moment."

Len was recommended by a friend after he was told by the medical specialists that he had a very serious malformation in the thalamus of his brain. The condition is called an arterio-venous malformation or AVM. There was a weakening in the walls of the blood vessels feeding this very intricate and important region of the brain and he was enduring terrible headaches and some numbness in his extremities. His doctors explained that the medical treatment for such a condition was gamma knife brain surgery. If he survived at all, he could have many cognitive deficits. If he did nothing, he left himself at risk of the malformation erupting and of inevitable sudden death. The odds were against him.

I was his last resort and our first meeting was brief. He was short on time and clearly short on inclination to believe in non-physical healing. He told me that he also had tendonitis from playing golf and wondered if I could do something for that, too. Before long he was soon on the massage table in a deep sleep-like state.

I thought things had gone well and after an hour brought him back. He said he felt unusually relaxed, yet he also seemed to be skeptical as to what he had just experienced. Not surprising for such a practical left brain thinking, alpha male. Still, he was very gracious and we said our farewells.

Sometimes, clients will call me soon after our sessions to let me know their good news. I hadn't heard from Len for several weeks and I was beginning to think that perhaps things had not gone so well for him, but then my phone rang. "Hi Philip, it's Len. I've been meaning to call you. The numbness in my extremities that I'd had for two years was gone the very next day after our session. Also, my stress was relieved and my tendonitis is completely gone too! Most importantly, I had another follow up MRI and the malformation has apparently shrunken from the size of a quarter to the size of a dime. The need for surgery has been averted."

The doctors apparently were astonished by the outcome. They said it was impossible.

Over the following year or two, I heard from Len asking for my assistance on a few other matters, including on behalf of a friend who had hurt her right shoulder ten years previously and could find no relief. She called me the very next day after that session. "I don't know what you did, but all the pain is now gone."

EPILEPSY

"I could black out at any time. I'll never drive or ride again."

Christine and I first met in a metaphysical/spiritual bookstore. We had lots in common and we became great friends. She is also into fitness and health, with a thriving home-based business on a ranch north of Toronto. In addition to caring for her animals, one of her greatest passions is driving a Harley Davidson. Recently, she had been experiencing epileptic seizures and was on strong medications to try and keep the unpredictable seizures under control. The prospect of no longer being able to drive or ride was a huge issue for her.

She was open to having some healing sessions, so I went to her ranch. Christine had three sessions, all of which went well. She now has a full and normal life, teaches yoga, and continues to ride her beloved Harley!

BLOCKED SALIVA GLAND

"I can't eat or drink. The pain is unbearable."

It was a bleak Monday evening in early December. The door opened slowly to reveal a tall, elegant young woman. I smiled and introduced myself and her eyes searched my face for a fleeting second, looking for…what? Hope, perhaps? With a wince of pain, she smiled back slightly.

We sat in her living room and, after exchanging pleasantries, she described her medical condition. Judy could not eat and could barely drink. On a pain and discomfort scale she was at a 10 plus. Her sub-mandible saliva gland duct was blocked with a large stone nearly 6mm (¼ inch) in size. The gland had also become infected. A prominent ENT (ear, nose, and throat) specialist had tried unsuccessfully in a two-hour operation to surgically remove the stone. She sought second opinions and all the ENTs had told her that the only medical recourse was to have her entire saliva gland removed. As a doctor herself she knew that a life without a saliva gland would also be intolerable, not to mention that there could also be permanent nerve damage to her face. She simply had to explore another avenue of possibility, no matter how outlandish it might seem, and thus the call to me.

Judy and I continued to speak at length about what was and had been going on in her life, recently and in the more distant past. A discomfort in her neck and jaw had been part of her life for nine years that seemed to worsen during emotional upset and stress. To me there was an obvious connection, but often the person suffering does not see it.

Judy seemed to be open to the possibility of non-physical healing, so after about 45 minutes we began. With some soothing music playing, I spoke quietly to her as she lay on my healing table. Slowly, she drifted away into a sleep-like state while I placed my hands gently on, around, and above her jaw, mouth, and neck. We ended our session and agreed to meet again in two days. I provided her with some positive thoughts and affirmations to focus on before our next session, that would allow the conscious and unconscious mind to do their parts to support the process further.

When we met again Judy's spirits seemed brighter and she was excited to report that the pain she had been experiencing had reduced significantly from a 10 to a more tolerable 4. She was no longer taking any Percocet for the pain. During our talk, Judy said that her concerns were now more with the blockage and swelling under her tongue and the discharge from the infection. She rated both of these as a 9 out of 10 on the misery scale.

I reminded Judy of the miraculous being she was already and emphasized that in each and every moment her physical body was performing millions and millions of complex functions without any conscious effort on her part. Her Essential Self was taking care of all these functions. I suggested that this is a part of her that is not generally known to the conscious mind, the ego, or intellect. On the table once again, she drifted off into a relaxed sleep-like state while the energies flowed gently and lovingly in and around her being. As we completed, we again agreed to meet in two days time.

On my third visit Judy told me that after our last meeting she had run to the bathroom and had to spit something out. Amazingly, she was also able to eat again! Judy was excited to tell me that the misery index for the swelling under her tongue and the infection was now only at a 2! The pain had gone. There was only a small bubble under her tongue and only a very slight discomfort on the left side of her neck.

I spoke to Judy a few weeks after that session. In the intervening time, she had had new x-rays that came back with the following reading: No calculi. The stone was completely gone!

ACID REFLUX

"For a long time I experienced the constant threat and misery of acid reflux disease."

Roy, a vital and distinguished gentleman, came to me at age 89. He had suffered with acid reflux for a long time, including a dreadful burning in his throat and stomach, and an appalling taste in his mouth. He had to be very careful about what and when he ate and would often be awakened during the night with great pain and discomfort. Roy's medical doctor had prescribed endless amounts of Gaviston pills for the symptoms but offered no actual remedy. The pills did little to relieve the unrelenting pain, discomfort, and burning sensation. The acidic, acrid taste in his mouth continued to be intolerable.

I asked Roy if he would like to have a healing session right there and then, where he stood chatting outside. He readily agreed (although he was concerned about what the neighbors might say!) I stood next to him and put my hand on his solar plexus and on his back. Right away, the energies began and I started to feel the familiar heat. We stood there for about 10 minutes and then we were complete.

The next day Roy reported that he had slept right through the entire night and that the burning feeling and taste was totally gone. In just one 10-minute session the condition completely disappeared!

It has been over a year now and Roy continues to be free of all the former acid reflux pain and discomfort and can pretty well eat whatever he likes.

"I'm overjoyed now to report that after just a few minutes with Philip, my discomfort has all but vanished!! It has truly been a life-changing experience for me. Philip is a miracle worker!"

SHOULDER AND NECK PAIN

"I don't know what you did, but my pain has been completely cured."

Whitney attended a special restorative yoga class of about a dozen people, where I was able to spend about six or seven minutes with each participant in a healing class setting. She reported that, in just those few minutes, I was able to completely heal her long-standing shoulder and neck problems.

KNEE PROBLEMS

"I can hardly walk, I can't skate. All my practice will be wasted."

Mary was a pre-teen figure skater. She had been unable to skate for some time due to a nasty fall. Her parents took her to physical therapists and specialists throughout the Toronto area with no success. Now, her father brought her to me, literally carrying her in. I spoke with Mary as she lay on a couch while her dad sat outside by the window enjoying the afternoon sun. As I spoke to her and put my hands on her knees and legs, she drifted off into a deep relaxation. After about an hour she was complete and said she felt as if she had been on a wonderful vacation and gave a vivid account of all kinds of beautiful colors while in this dream-like state. The next day, her parents were dumbfounded as they watched her perform skating jumps with ease.

Mary said, "After I saw you, I could walk again, and the very next day I was actually doing figure skating jumps for the first time in five months. I am not going to miss the nationals after all. Thank you so much!"

TEETH AND ROOT CANAL

"I have terrible tooth pain. Another root canal will cost me thousands!"

Over the years, Clare had had a number of painful and expensive root canals. Recently, the pain began again and her dentist recommended yet another. Clare had received a number of healing sessions from me for other health and wellness concerns and, when I asked her, said she was open to trying some healing on her jaw and teeth as well.

As she lay back deeply relaxed on her couch, I gently cradled her right jaw and touched her lower molars. After about an hour, we were complete and the next day, the pain had gone. Clare cancelled the root canal procedure with her dentist and is problem-free to this day. In just one session we eliminated the pain and we eliminated the issue.

FOOT PROBLEMS

"I'm afraid my life is over."

Hanna had severe foot problems and was not able to walk properly. Her job of 25 years required her to be mobile and on her feet all day so this issue was completely debilitating. When we met, I spoke to Hanna and explained to her about the strength and power of non-physical energies. I touched her arm and heart. After that the pain in Hanna's feet went away.

Hanna says, "I thought my life was over because I could not walk. If I couldn't walk I would not be able to work. Now I can walk pain-free again. You are my savior! I am so grateful. Thank you!"

CHEST PAIN AND FIBROID TUMORS

"All my life I have been in pain. Now, I feel wonderful."

Kaitlin is a nurse. She had experienced severe and unrelenting pain in her upper chest all her life. There was no known medical cause found, even after every type of medical test had been conducted. She also had dreadful pain in her lower abdomen due to two inoperable fibroid tumors. After her first healing session, the pain in her upper chest left completely. After the second, the intolerable pain in her lower abdomen disappeared.

Kaitlin says, "Now I feel wonderful! Thank you!"

There are, of course, many, many more anecdotes covering almost every imaginable type of malady, but this is all the room we have for now. As the authority on energy healing, I hope that you have found this chapter to be helpful as an introduction to such an expansive metaphysical topic. The concepts may be new to you, although the principles have always been used, in every part of the world, throughout history.

If you feel that I may be able to assist you or a loved one, please call me in Toronto at 416-447-9550. If there is a good fit with us and we do work together, I will visit you in the privacy of your own home and I will commit to working with you until you are completely well again. In the meantime, may blessings of Love and Light always be upon you.

Thank you for your interest! You can learn more at www.PhilipYoungHealer.com

Honor Your Inner Treasures

CELINA TIO

COLLECTIVE CREATED ME

"We are all created from our experiences, and the first step towards embracing our inner treasures is to acknowledge this. You are wonderful, and the experiences that took you to this point are all part of that. Do not be afraid of yourself; instead, let yourself shine." This quote is from my recent book, *Honor Your Inner Treasures*. It's an underlying principle of that work, and its message is most certainly applicable to what you're about to read in this chapter of *The Authorities*. Collective Created Me explains in the *Honor Your Inner Treasures* book, how most of our beliefs are obtained through training and repetition, and assumed personality through education. Becoming aware of the Collective Created Me is extremely beneficial because it puts you on the road to self-acceptance and realization, forgiveness, independence, appreciation and true happiness.

Think about this for a moment: do you remember someone in your family being sick when you were a child? Were the hours spent in family time talking about symptoms, where pain started, where it ended, how long it lasted, and medicines? It's likely that much of the conversation also revolved around nurses, doctors' assessments and trips to the hospital. Soon, with so much health and sickness related information taken in, you unconsciously started to become so familiar enough with that illness that you accepted it as just part of your family. It became so normal that you could quickly respond to questions about it as if it were your illness, too. "My uncle Charlie had it, and so did his son and my grandmother. It runs in our family."

Imagine if the conversation you heard about Uncle Charlie's illness had been about the way that healthy habits, physical activities, and letting go of toxic thoughts helped him recover. What would you have learned to do then in the event of an illness?

This example of negativity changing your perspective is applicable to other life experiences. What about love and relationships? Conversations about unfaithfulness, divorce, unhealthy relationships, abuse, violence? How has the negativity of those conversations affected your beliefs and the actions you've taken in life? Money is another example. People often say they never have enough money. Stories are shared about someone's new business failing, or friends who've lost their homes because they couldn't make their mortgage payments. Wouldn't stories of success have a more positive impact to encourage others to improve in their lives?

Most people receive diagnoses during their lives pertaining to health, personal finances, the country's economy, beauty, fashion and relationships. Usually, these diagnoses are fully accepted as truth and fact. There is an alternative, however. Why not see a diagnosis as feedback of that exact, precise moment and utilize it as the moment of opportunity to change, to create, to expand, to become, to discover, is opening up for you?

People often say when a door closes a window opens, and wait for the window to open right in front of them. Often, hoping that the window will magically pop open and the situation will change. The sad thing is, it may take a while and in the meantime the beliefs that life is not fair, life is hard or life is good to others start to run your thoughts.

I want you to know that all windows and doors are always open for you. Even more, there are no windows, there are no doors, because once you embrace your greatness you are free to live with purpose.

Going back to our example of listening to other people's life experiences, can you perceive how your fears and beliefs originated during these events? The occasions are wonderful moments to enjoy and remember the past, but sometimes people retell stories about illnesses with as much detail as they can recall. It's possible the now-adult children have no recollection of the event's seriousness because they remember with a child's naïveté only how happy they were about recovery. Now, listening to the story of an experience in your life that evoked sadness, these adults inevitably feel pulled down and relive that low-energy feeling. You can change that feeling in you and all the people around you. Next time you are at a reunion be sure to evoke moments that bring joy and laughter. Everyone will leave feeling great, having enjoyed the party, and with a more positive attitude for the next adventure in their life.

BECOME AWARE - CONNECT WITH YOUR INNER BEING

Let go of the stories and let go of others' experiences. Start living your own.

Embrace the belief that your life is complete and absolute just as is. Take a deep breath, aware of your body, starting at the top and working your way down. Begin with your scalp, your hair, your temples, your forehead, your eyebrows, your eyes, then move on until you reach the tip of your toes. It's important to take in every part of yourself so don't stop at the surface. Recognize your organs and their functions, even noting your breath as it travels into your lungs and fills you with pure oxygen. Become aware of your being. I ask that you become aware of your being, not that you look into the mirror or take a selfie and analyze it to see if you have wrinkles, or criticize your body shape. Stop judging yourself and start knowing yourself.

Selfies have become, to many, a tool to prove oneself, or a tool of confirmation of existence, presence and self-acceptance, and others' approval of the moment that is being lived.

As if the moment being lived needs external approval to be considered as a "perfect moment" and only then sharing it with the world.

When you look at the moment you are living as an image that "looks good" or "like happiness", the gap between what you are doing "looks great", and truly feeling great, is large. There is no enjoyment or happiness if it always depends on others' opinions. Making a picture look good when the emotions you are feeling at the moment don't match the illusion of the created image is keeping you from living a true honest happy moment.

Different from this is taking a picture to capture a moment of real pleasure and happiness, and the peace and joy that healthy relationships and celebrations bring. Those are photographs that recall true emotions of happiness, in turn aligning your whole being into feeling truly amazing. These selfies are not only a moment taken with a camera; they are taken into your soul, leaving a long-lasting impression in your life. Those are moments that you will truly love to share with others without deleting anything. What is your selfie telling you when you look at it? What is that image revealing?

Become aware of yourself and the moment without editing. Be completely honest about everything. In this moment of self-awareness, accept everything – your age, aches, sadness, longings, best memories, dreams – without shyness, even if they look too big at this moment. Become aware because for the first time in your life you will be truly, honestly and entirely present with yourself, as you know yourself to be at this moment. What is your inner self telling you? This is the true SELF you should be contemplating.

If you do this, for the first time in your life you will be truly, honestly and entirely present. Your unique, true self will be revealed. For many people, doing this will be the scariest meeting of their lives. To me it is the most amazing!

When working with my clients, this point of their journey is the most exciting to me. As their guide to reaching their true inner being throughout the Honor Your Inner Treasures™ Program, the transformation the client undergoes is magical, because their life suddenly expands as they embrace and accept fully their inner self.

YOUR EMOTIONS ARE POWERFUL. LEARN FROM THEM.

Pretending is the only sure thing someone does when they are denied their true feelings. Pretending to feel well, smiling just with the movement of the facial muscles, repeating clichés as a consolation to true feelings, and distancing ourselves from loved ones or hiding from life aren't effective measures. Not talking about problems doesn't solve them. On the contrary, the repetition of those actions and inner messages undoubtedly becomes the reality in your life, which extends the sadness, insecurity, lack of confidence, and low-energy life. It's an unhealthy cycle, difficult to break. Have you ever heard people complaining about the good luck of others, or blaming the sad circumstances in their life on other people's lives? If you come close to a person behaving this way, stay away. You don't want to adopt that attitude.

You can change, you can become more, and you can be the best amazing you because you truly, genuinely feel it. Sharing your life with others with honesty, because there is absolutely nothing to hide, is liberating. Accept that you are a human being experiencing life, and in the process are growing, becoming, expanding, and evolving.

Through this process there will be moments that call for change, whether of habits, beliefs, actions, or behaviors. Change is a process of evolving into a different state. The emotions that you carry through the transition are of most importance. Are you making the change out of resentment or fear? Is it happening because you don't feel you're enough? Or are you just resigning yourself because you are obedient to unhappiness. What if you make the change because you know that you would love and enjoy doing something different?

Ask yourself what you need to make this change? Maybe it's taking a course or learning something new. Going through training is a fun ride when all you are doing is acquiring new skills to master what you love to do! Don't let the fear of change keep you from becoming healthier and happier. You look and feel healthy and beautiful when you are enjoying the moments that you are creating in your life. Change gives you jolts of energy that propels you to do more.

CHANGE TO THE POSITIVE SIDE OF LIFE

"Change the thinking positive and acting negative attitude." – Celina Tio

I hear people talking about difficult situations in their lives that end with usual comments like "I'm staying positive," "I'm trying to think positive" or "Hopefully…" However, simply repeating the mantra "I'm staying positive" does not make it true. When you are vibrating in the true sense of positive energy your life has no room for negative energy. Positive will always see, hear, understand, interpret, and plan in a constructive manner. When clients come for their first consultations with me, I listen attentively to their voices. From their tones I can hear the negative energy of unhealed wounds, regardless of the words they use. They tell their stories as if they've become comfortable hurting. This is a common means of self-defense and emotional survival.

In their journeys through the Honor Your Inner Treasures™ Program, clients delve into their true selves and are guided through the process of transmuting their thoughts into a positive perspective. This transformation occurs once we do the necessary inner work at the soul level, which is the purest essence of being. Anger may become understanding and compassion; resentment an opportunity for self-reflection and inner growth; and solitude a time of self-forgiveness and self-acceptance. The more you discover about your inner being, the closer you are to the positive energy of your true self. Knowing that each step my clients take brings them closer to their inner being of positive creation gives me great joy. It is important to create life experiences in such a way that, when you reflect on the past, all you see is a magical garden of your own design that you can be proud of having imagined, lived, grown and created.

Let's do an exercise that will assist you with looking at decisions based on fear. You will need to sit comfortably on a chair and have with you a pad of paper and a pen. Imagine an "X" mark on the floor to your right that represents the change that you want to make, and an "X" to your left side. The "X" mark on the left side represents the negative reasons that you have to make the change in your life and the "X" on the right side represents positive ones.

On the paper write the reasons you want to make the change. For example, let's say that the decision you want to make is about a change in career. Write on the paper the thoughts that have crossed your mind. Use one piece of paper per thought about the issue. (It is important to follow these steps carefully.) Now, decide if the thought you've written is negative or positive and put the paper to your left or right side. Use the guide on page 9 to help you determine whether your thoughts are positive or negative.

As you can see, on the column for thoughts I have underlined the negative comments. On the fourth example the word but is underlined because the "buts" are so big in our lives. You truly have to listen closely when you speak. Until you change your internal dialogue and are able to do this spontaneously, it is best to do this exercise by writing it on pieces of paper. Doing this will change the thinking positive and acting negative attitude that most people have without realizing why their lives are so difficult. Once you have identified your thought process about the issue, you can transform it and move all your thoughts to the positive side.

When you finish transforming your thought process, written now with only positive reasons, you will feel much more enthusiastic and energized to move forward and take the necessary steps to become or do. Every step of the way becomes more pleasurable because you have created a happy and positive future for yourself. What seemed to be big obstacles in the road are now the building stones and success is within reach! Congratulations! You truly do have the inner power to transform your life.

I have created a transformational workbook for my clients that enter the Honor Your Inner Treasures™ Program and as we go through the process they do simple, fun and motivating change processes. When they finish, only then the realization comes regarding how powerful it is to invest time into loving ourselves.

BELIEFS

All people have beliefs that help structure their lives. We know with great certainty that whatever we believe is true, and one of these beliefs is self-worth. People even determine their income based on their belief of self-worth. Your resume indicates exactly how much money you will make in the next year. When you review it and no changes have been made, you are hoping that inflation or the economy of the company you work for will determine the increase in the salary that you will be earning. Have you ever stopped to think about it? You are giving your power to another person to determine your growth, not only in your economy, but also your personal potential to do more, to become who you want to be.

I have worked with clients who are business owners feeling stressed out because of low funds, poor self-esteem and a lack of confidence. These issues not only impact their personal lives but also how their business grows. Those negative beliefs, ideas and limitations also have an impact on their earnings and the status of their finances, and all the people working for their company.

I remember working with Priti, a 43-year-old married woman. She emigrated to Canada from India, where she had received her degree as a software engineer. Once in Canada, Priti was able to obtain a position where she could use some of her education and experience. The reason I say 'some' of her education and experience is because when she came to see me for the first time she said that she was starting to feel bored with her job and not living up to her full potential. Priti felt that there were problems in the company that took too long to solve and required great work to make operations run more efficiently. Doing things the way the company had done for years was causing the same problems over and over again. She wanted to make a change and had a vision to do so.

However, Priti was quiet and didn't like to be the center of attention, so she kept to herself, trying to fit into the company's mold. Eventually, the conflict between shyness and wanting to change operations caused her a great deal of stress. She could not feel confident putting forth her suggestions. And although there was nothing I could do to help her with her software issues, I was able to help her build her confidence to act, speak, think and move forward. With those new positive traits, she was able to increase her self-esteem and recognize her own value.

Being foreign and fearing she might appear ignorant to others was one of Priti's greatest stumbling blocks. To offset this, I offered a metaphor. I asked her to consider the plastic casing that envelops the computer containing the software she created. Is that foreign? Obviously, the answer is no. The casing is just another part of the whole computer just as she, too, is part of the whole.

In creation nothing is foreign. We are all co-creating contributing our energy into the amazing universe we all live in. This is why it is so important that you truly live your lives from your inner treasures because underneath your fears and doubts you are pure potential, everyone has amazing positive energy to add to the whole.

We also worked on Priti's self-esteem and confidence by training her subconscious mind to act, feel and think the way the leader she desired to be would. The leader she wanted to be was one who confidently and clearly communicated her views, ideas and solutions with the tone of a manager. In just a few weeks Priti noticed she was expressing her ideas, asking questions and sharing her knowledge and experience without feeling timid. Most importantly, she noticed that her peers welcomed her ideas.

Eventually, Priti realized this company didn't have potential to grow and she was putting all of her potential in a box too small for her. She knew she was ready to move on with confidence.

That spark of inner realization of your personal self, and of how truly valuable your contribution is to everything you do, changes everything. You become confident to plan and live your life making decisions that feel right, and feel an inner peace because you gained control. Now, you have the power to do the things that are truly important to you. Once you learn to expand your consciousness beyond your fear, the limitation you had becomes limit-less.

In my upcoming book, *Limitless Beliefs - 7 Steps to Transcend into a Joyful and Abundant You*, you will find the how-to for this process. To purchase, learn more about the book, www.limitlessbeliefs.com or www.celinatioauthor.com.

YOUR LIFE IS YOUR DECISION AND YOUR CREATION

"Create your life experiences in such a way that the day you look back all you see is a magical garden of your own design that you can be proud of having imagined,

lived, grown and created." – Celina Tio

"Really? Are you sure? Because I was told…" These are all comments based on a lack of confidence. This does not have to be you! You are able to declare your independence, power and freedom! To embrace the true and pure intention of creation!

I'll share with you the experience of Laura, a beautiful and intelligent woman who came to my office for help. As she introduced herself and explained the reason why she had made the appointment, I was amazed. At 32 years old, she was a successful fashion designer. Her passion, however, was singing and songwriting. What an amazing girl, and what a disparity in her professional career compared to her dreams.

Her narrative was sad due to many of her life's circumstances and events. Her self-esteem and confidence was at an all-time low after ending a relationship that was going nowhere. Now, she hoped to let go of all her little self. Laura wanted to have more confidence to make decisions and communicate her ideas and feelings, and she wanted to feel good about herself. Simply put, she wanted to live happily.

I could have told her how beautiful, amazing and intelligent I thought she was. I could have pointed out all the wonderful opportunities she could have in life or how much I admired her. But she wasn't there for me to tell her what most any friend would. She needed to know from her own heart, discovering and loving herself so that she could go through her life's journey knowing her essence.

At the end of her journey I asked Laura to write what she decided was most valuable about herself. She took a few days and sent me an e-mail describing her value as she perceived it. Imagine the courage it took to be so vulnerable. Without relying on anyone else's opinions, she confessed her own beauty, strength, warmth and intelligence. She had honored her inner treasures.

I have asked her permission to share this with you because I want you to know that it is also possible for you. She kindly and happily agreed because she felt she could help other people. Maybe that person today is you or someone you love.

"I value myself because I am a strong person who perseveres through hardship, and I have faith I will get through it. I value myself because I am loving and kind-hearted person. I value myself because I take care of those in need and treat them just as I would treat myself. I value myself because I am a hard worker and very motivated. I value myself because I am a good woman. I value myself because I have self-respect and integrity, and will not allow anyone to take that away. I value myself because I am humble in life. I value myself because I am a good sister, friend, daughter, and lover because I care for people's feelings. I value myself because of my relationship with God and how I want to continue to help myself be better. I value myself because I am a loving woman who shares love with everyone. I value myself because I can make people laugh and really bring out the best in them; this shows me how amazing I am. I value myself because even if I am scared or fearful I have courage to face those fears. I value myself because of my ability to forgive and make amends even when people have truly hurt me. I value my positive thinking and my ability to turn what can be a bad situation into a great one. I value myself because I am able to express my feelings and my emotions now in a calm and mature way. I value myself because any goal I set for myself I achieve, because I am willing to work hard. I value myself because I always keep on smiling even when the going gets tough. I value myself because I am beautiful, strong, smart, mature, funny, loving, and kind person."

- Laura, Toronto, Canada
Fashion Designer/ Singer and Songwriter, naturally from the heart.

APPRECIATION

If life were a coin, would you say it is less valuable when you are looking on the head side just because the imprinted value is on the other side and you can't see it?

The value of everything is found through deep appreciation. Lots of people walk through life with the expectation of being accepted and liked by others, but they suffer a great deal when the world around them doesn't show them what they expect. Start increasing your self-value by appreciating your life as it is in this moment. Even if your world looks or feels different than you'd like, there is value to be found. You can increase that value by describing it and saying thank you. At first, it might take some creativity if you have been depreciating things most of your life.

Let's think of something you do every day, like eating. All of us eat when we are hungry, but some also eat when anxious, nervous or depressed. There is even a name for this: comfort food. Comfort food is supposed to make you feel better when you eat it; however, nobody has ever said, "I was feeling sad and I ate a whole bowl of ice cream and now everything is fine! All of a sudden I feel loved and my finances have improved drastically with every spoonful of food I ate!" This would simply not be true.

On the other hand, when you eat because you feel hungry your body and mind feel better because they receive the nourishment needed. If you offer and share your meal and spend time in the company of family or friends, your soul is nourished as well. In preparing your meal, be grateful that you have the ingredients on hand needed to prepare the meal that will nourish every cell in your body. Imagine all the minerals, vitamins, proteins, carbohydrates and fibers that are present in what you are about to consume, and how you are benefiting from them. Thank the supermarket for having them available for you, and the people who've dedicated their life into growing them. Even thank the work you do that earns you the funds to buy your food. It's crucial to become aware of the dimension of what you are about to eat.

- Be grateful to the soil that has the perfect nutrients to grow your food.
- Be grateful to the sun and the water for adding their energy.
- Be grateful to the universe for having created a planet that contains everything you need.
- Be grateful for the beauty of the colors, textures and aromas of the vegetables, herbs or fruits, or a cup of coffee.
- Be grateful to the person who will share this meal with you.
- Be grateful that you can share your moment with that person and have each other's company.
- Be grateful that you have the ability to offer and share your meal.
- Be grateful that life is allowing this moment to sit, rest, replenish, keep each other's company and share whatever it is that needs to be shared at the moment.

By now, appreciation has started to flow from the heart and you will know if what you are about to eat is healthy for you. If you have to thank the chemicals named on the package that are so difficult to pronounce instead of the natural sweet aroma of a natural ripe tomato, you will know not to eat it. Your body will show you resistance. When appreciation flows from the heart, you will feel true comfort even when you drink plain water. Do it at your next meal. Do the same with your home, your family, your pet and your neighbor.

Practicing heartfelt appreciation will change your perspective on life.

SELF-REALIZATION

"You have the power of pure energy within you to be, to do, to have, to accomplish, to become your dream." – Celina Tio

When you truly know your essence, everything changes easily. Your relationships are healthier by helping you grow with people who share your life's path. Life becomes pleasurable and enjoyable, and conflict and stress no longer emanate from you. You understand that ego makes peoples lives sad and full of problems, and that it drives competition, fear, war and destruction.

Knowing your essence also means the things that you're doing now are in line with what makes you feel happy. It's easy to identify if you're off balance because life no longer feels whole. You become aware of your energy and how it affects everything around you. You have a fresh understanding that you are part of creation, co-creating with all that makes us one.

You become more independent when you know your essence, investing into your wellbeing and happiness instead of things that have no value to your personal self. Rich and wealthy has a whole different meaning now. No more spending to do things or obtain things just because you feel bored or empty. You'll no longer feel the need to shop in an attempt to feel happy or, even worse, to look happy. You become independent and know that you are the only one responsible for how you are living your life, with no one else to blame. Vacationing to escape from reality is a thing of the past. Instead, you'll have the freedom to choose a destination that will give you enjoyment in everything from the planning to the adventure to the return.

At this point, inner peace has become real in your life and you'll have the self-realization that you truly are the creator of every moment in your life. Your future is right this moment, so make it amazing and wonderful. Move from the comfort spot of sameness, obedience and unhappiness. Walking on your self-pity will take you only to more of the same. It is time to tell yourself that you deserve to experience life, and to savor and indulge in the sweetness and pure love of creation. You deserve to feel free of unnecessary pain, have inner peace and feel truly loved.

Of course we all have sad moments in our lives. It is normal to experience loss and birth, laughter with tears of joy and also tears of sadness, and expansion and contraction. It is the Yin and Yang of life. What's important is what you do with it.

Your inner being has been waiting for you to listen truthfully to the pureness within. You are powerful beyond your comprehension, and have more than strength. You have the power of pure energy within you to be, to do, to have, to accomplish, and to become your dream. When I realized how powerful I was created to be, I stopped feeling small. I rid myself of unnecessary fears, choosing instead to be one with the moment. I learned to breathe moments out of love, peace and joy, and to share it with you and everyone around me. Let me help you heal. Allow me to guide you into that place of discovering and once and for all Honor Your Inner Treasures. Your life will be transformed.

www.honoryourinnertreasures.com

www.limitlessbeliefs.com

www.celinatioauthor.com

The Secret to Words

JACQUELINE LUCIEN

When you first learned to read, you probably were taught to associate each letter with an object and a sound. It was pretty flat-footed, like "A" is for apple or "B" is for ball. The things your parents or teachers used to illustrate the sound represented by each letter may have made sense to you? Did you ever wonder what the letters originally stood for, *or if they stood for anything* or how someone came up with their specific shapes and curves?

Each letter we use today has a rich and fascinating, multi-layered meaning. Each has a history of associations that make it just about perfect in terms of its shape and design. Just like Chinese and Japanese characters, each letter of the alphabet represents so much more than just a sound — it tells a story and conveys the ancient and original meaning in a powerful way which influences our words today. So, how did these letters that mean so much in our daily lives come to be in the first place?

We all know the old saying that a picture is worth a thousand words. Well, it's true and nowhere more so than when talking about the letters we use to read and write. The alphabet is connected to ancient pictures, and the essence of those pictures comes from both concrete objects and abstract ideas. If a picture is worth a thousand words, and letters (in their ancient essence) are pictures, *what is the worth of one letter? What is the worth of one word?*

THE CREATION OF THE ROMAN ALPHABET

The Roman alphabet (the 26 letters from A to Z used to create the English language) originated in Ancient Egypt. (The Romans influenced, and were influenced, by many cultures.) The Egyptian form of writing is called *"Mdu Ntr," Medu Neter or the hieroglyphics of KMT, which means the Language of the Gods.* The characters, sometimes called ideographs, pictographs or phonograms, are symbols or pictures used to represent sounds or words. From these Ancient Egyptian hieroglyphs, letters were created. Each letter shape can be traced back to a hieroglyph, and the hieroglyph itself (or its meaning) can be directly connected to the way in which we use that letter on a daily basis.

How wonderful it would be for me to regale you with a story about the origin of each of our 26 Roman letters, but that would take a whole book — and that is something for another time. Instead, let's focus on the Roman letters A, B, D, and P, as well as the connection between the Gods and letters "G" and "N." The origins of these letters range from simple to complex, and provide a broad view of how the Roman alphabet came to be.

 A IS FOR "APED/VULTURE

It is fairly safe to say that the letter "A" is one of, if not, the first letter children learn. As I mentioned, it is highly likely that a child first learns "A is for apple". What that child doesn't get taught is that "A" stands for lots of other things that actually better relate to the letter itself. After all, an A is a high reaching letter coming to a point; a round apple looks nothing like an A.

In ancient times, for example, a child might have been told "A is for aped." The Egyptian word "aped" is represented by a hieroglyph of a bird; and translates to the scientific word for bird (more specifically, vulture). The vulture ("aped") has a bad reputation these days, but was originally known for being a high-flying bird that valiantly cared for its young. The aped was also considered the Pharaoh's favorite bird. Clearly, the aped had a high station in the culture, making it a great choice for the first letter of the alphabet.

Digging deeper, let's look at the qualities represented by the letter A itself, and how those qualities are related to the aped. The A is reminiscent of pyramids; it is a triangle with great heights. Further, the aped is linked to words like "Air"… "Altitude"… "Ascend" … "Appreciate" — words that all have meanings connected to greatness, height and direction. These words' meanings, coupled with the fact that the letter A is represented by a distinct and greatly appreciated bird, are all indicators of why the capital letter A itself is visually tall and reminiscent of height.

There is a second 'glyph' represented by an arm, thus the word arm. And, for example, it is the "a" in leverage. Thus, one would have to make a distinction between which glyph is represented in the word in question. This will be elaborated further in my book, along with many other examples.

Further, the great Egyptian God Amun, an incredibly influential and powerful God, is later called "Amen," the same word used by many religions to end a prayer. The importance of the A is so great that it is used, in part, to finalize the hopes and thoughts of multitudes of people to ensure that they are heard and responded to by their equivalent of the great Egyptian God Amun. Jumping ahead, Amun is an ascended / high and wise/seeing god.

B IS FOR BARE FOOT

In continuing with our exploration into letter origins, let's look at the letter "B". It originates from the hieroglyph of a bare foot. Among the first qualities we can associate with a bare foot is down (or downward) as the bare foot is at the bottom, or base, of the body. (Can you see a pattern emerging?) The bare foot is support for the body, like a brace or the base of a table. The bare foot helps with movement, bringing you to where you need to be. "Bottom"… "Base"… "Brace"… "Bring"… These words indicate support in both stillness and movement.

The letter B itself is sturdy. The bottom, larger than the top, stabilizes the letter, holding the letter upright, just as the bare foot holds up the rest of the body. When we look at the shape of the lowercase "b," we see its appearance is very similar to that of a leg and barefoot. Other examples of how the letter shows up in our language include: "Boots on the ground" and "Battalion," both representing foot soldiers.

D IS FOR DIGITS/HAND

The letter "D" originated from the hieroglyphic symbol of a hand. The Egyptian word for hand is drrt , The function of the hand (because of our opposable thumbs) separates man from the animals. Man does many things with his hand(s). Among the words that start with D, and are connected to the hieroglyph, is the word "digits," i.e., the fingers of the hand. Digits help man "Do" things... "Duty"... "Drive"... "Diligence." These words are all connected to man doing and accomplishing something. Even more closely linked to the letter D and the hieroglyph of the hand are words such as "dexterous" and "dexterity." The meanings of these words are directly related to hands and the ability of the hand to perform tasks. Thus, D has the quality of action and is directly related to the action of the hand. *Even though the English word hand does not start with the letter d its meaning is consistent in the word.*

▢ P IS FOR PORTAL/DOOR

You may be wondering why I chose to jump all the way to "P" at this point. It's because of the very interesting connection between two letters that I want to share with you. The Egyptian hieroglyph for "P" is a square, more specifically, a door. Now, think about the letter D again. If you were to turn the lowercase letter "d" around (by 180 degrees), what would you have? Yes! A small letter "p"! The d in the picture of the door that we see in the hieroglyph is truly a p, as in the word "Portal." I also looked across languages in Spanish you have puerta.

While it might not be your first thought, when considering doors or portals, we are truly thinking of going out into an open space or a place that affords opportunity (opportunity having the double-p, or two portals... even the word "port" is embedded in "opportunity"). The letter P is instrumental in many common sayings, including, "When opportunity knocks, answer the door" and "window of opportunity." These sayings allude to the double-p (two portals) in opportunity, and the door or portal at which to respond to the opportunity being given to you. So the quality of a door to be considered is that it is an opening, something you can go through. The words that come to mind are: passage...privilege...progress....port....peer (as in look through).

THE LETTERS OF THE GODS

A deeper analysis of letters and hieroglyphs reveals the remarkable way in which some letters correlate with the ancient Gods worshipped by the Egyptians. To appreciate the connection between the two you need to know a bit about Egyptian Cosmology.

Cosmology in general is the study of origins and the universe. Egyptian cosmology revolves around the required balance between humans and the Gods. Humans believed that if they were cooperative, kind and just to one another, the Gods would, in turn, be kind and keep the forces of nature in balance. There are many Gods in Egyptian Cosmology: The God of the ground/earth (Geb), the God of the night/sky (Goddess Nut), the God of the sun (Re), the God of air (Shu) and the God of chaos (Nu). I'm going to focus on the first two Gods, Geb and Nut, for the next part of our journey through the alphabet.

G IS FOR GEB

The letter "G" comes from the hieroglyphic letter or symbol for the stool. In this respect, the stool is defined as a stand upon which you put a jar. That definition suggests support, foundation, and a most telling word, "grounding" (the stool is on the ground). The "G" also represents the Egyptian God, Geb. As previously mentioned, Geb is the God of earth itself. Egyptian cosmology states that Geb is quite literally the earth... the "ground"... the "geography"... the "globe". The earth "gives" and supports life. The earth "grows; "it generates." As a result, it makes perfect sense for the letter "G" to come out of a symbol that represents an object that grounds and supports, and is the foundation for other objects and beings. Geb is also shown supporting or holding up Nut, the night/sky. Geb is Nut's husband/brother. Does that give you something to consider regarding the ancient wisdom for the need to support?

⋀⋁⋀⋁⋀ N IS FOR NUT

The letter "N" originated from the hieroglyph of wavy lines, similar to waves and water. Some say that N represents water, which is a source of life. Also, similar to the letter G, the Roman letter N is connected to both Egyptian hieroglyphs and the Egyptian Gods.

In Egyptian Cosmology, there is the Goddess Nut. She gave birth to the sun, and the sun revolves around her body in a 24-hour cycle to make night and day. Nut is commonly depicted as a woman who is arched over the earth (Geb) on hands and feet. The Goddess Nut is representative of the barrier between chaos and the cosmos and is seen as a protector of the dead whom she keeps with her in her starry sky.

The Goddess Nut is the night, the darkness from which everything derives. In English, she is the "Night". In Spanish, she is the "Noche"... in French "Nuit"... in Greek "Nyx" ... Nacht in German ... "Nox" in Latin ... in Sanskrit

"Naktam" and in Hindi "Nishaa."

"Nyx" (Ancient Greek: Νυξ, "night")" in the Latin translation is the Greek goddess, or personification,of the night. A shadowy figure, Nyx stood at or near the beginning of creation and was the mother of other personified Gods such as Hypnos (Sleep) and Thánatos (Death). Nyx's appearances in mythology are few and far between, but what has been revealed about her is that she is a figure of exceptional power and beauty. Nyx is found in the shadows of the world and is only ever seen in glimpses. As you get away from the source, the object or concept can gain other interpretations.

When we see the reference to Nut as protector of death, it represents that, as time went on, words that were powerful from the opposite quality. The words that come to mind are Engish "no" ... Spanish "nada," ...german "nicht", " nein"

I urge you to continue with your own exploration of the word "night", its spellings and meanings across languages. It is unlikely that the Gods from one belief system to the next can be so similar in both names and existence without it being anything less than purposeful.

So… what does all of this Goddess Nut and Night talk have to do with the Roman letter N? Well, the letter N is derived directly from Nut. And, again, Nut is the night, a bringer of life (like the water depicted in the hieroglyph), and the protector of the dead. Nut's role is natural and nurturing. Nut is the N in origin, beginning, expansive and garden. She is the N in neuter, as she was disempowered through time and forgotten for her role as giving birth to the son. And, what about the word "not" representing further neutralization and negation? As you look at how she is depicted, with her arching body, you can see she is the N in expansive beginning and origin. She is also the N in the words span and extend over or across something, like space and time.

The capital letter N looks physically similar to the waves in the hieroglyph. Interestingly, the depiction of Nut in her arched form is also similar in shape to the lowercase Roman "n". These connections between Roman letters, hieroglyphs, and Ancient Egyptian Gods cannot be ignored or thrown aside. These connections are very much real.

Ok, I Can See It. But Why Should I Care?

While reading thus far, have you said to yourself, "this may be interesting, but how can I use this information?" Or, are you thinking that this chapter satisfies a little curiosity, but that's it; you'll move on to something else because this information does not have any real purpose for you. How can you actually use this in your life?

Doesn't this understanding of letters make them seem so much more alive? Have you not gained a greater appreciation for the letters we use to construct our most meaningful of words? Consider for just a moment how much more enlightening the learning of the Roman alphabet could be to a five-year-old child if he or she were taught by way of hieroglyphics, meaning and origin. The very nature of learning would be greatly enhanced.

Children would not only learn what each hieroglyphic and Roman letter looks like, but would also understand their meanings. Learning the origin of each letter provides the opportunity to more fully grasp the how and why of each shape and sound, as well as the connection of these shapes and sounds to the bigger piece reading words as a whole. Further, understanding each letter's origin enhances the learning of vocabulary and spelling by making connections with the meaning of letters and the purpose each holds within a word. The more we use our five senses to learn, the more mastery we can have. *Children could be encouraged to put letters together to create their own words, another form of creativity and another way to tell their story. I invite you to consider additional uses for this information.*

BUT I'M BEYOND LEARNING TO READ

Pictures provide a very profound way to anchor learning and memory. Further, pictures and words, particularly when they work together, are exceptionally useful tools for drawing you in to a subject. Graphic artists are taught to come up with abstract ideas and create logos to convey meaning, (the same thought process used to create the hieroglyphics) while advertisers use words and pictures to gain access to your mind and influence your perception.

As an example, let's talk about the soda 7UP®. Would the brand name affect you the same way if it were 7b? (The b that is downward and associated with the bare foot.) No, of course it wouldn't, because, in its essence, 7b is a "downer." So, instead, we are sold 7UP, which includes the letter P associated with an upward door, an opening and an *opportunity* for something. The brand name 7UP is pure genius. Without the understanding and purpose of our letters, we are unable to understand the cause and effect of what we are seeing.

Also, by unlocking the meaning of letters, you can cross check the dictionary or encyclopedia and go beyond the history of the words, the etymology to understand how letters and words interact with each other. What are the letters really saying? Why is it that a word can mean something in one language, but mean something completely different in another language? When you explore the reference tools I just mentioned, you see that the meaning of a word changes according to the culture and powers that be at the time. Now you have the tools to see how the story of the letters supports the dictionary meaning, or not, and why.

Learning occurs in stages; since this is an introduction I chose words to represent the concepts presented, primarily having the letter at the beginning of the word. Once there is a command of the concept you begin to see its function in any part of the word.

Further, we can empower children by providing them with an understanding of the meanings and origins of the letters in their names. We can challenge them to personify each letter and gain strength, courage and leadership skills based on the history associated with their names. The big picture impact is that we can teach children to read and write with this new perspective. We can use the origin and meaning of letters to create logos and company names that are more powerful and impactful than ever before. We can provide another efficient way to remember names by seeing what the letters in the name say. We can advance into the future by using the keys provided by our world's ancient history and earliest writing.

If you would like more information about hieroglyphics in general, or want to learn more about the meaning of a specific letter or word, like your name, please feel free to contact me at jahkey2@yahoo.com.

www.ingramcontent.com/pod-product-compliance
Lightning Source LLC
Chambersburg PA
CBHW050641160426
43194CB00010B/1765